Ghosts of Kenosha

Beth Cooper

Schiffer Publishing Ltd®

4880 Lower Valley Road, Atglen, Pennsylvania 19310

Other Schiffer Books on Related Subjects
Haunted Kansas City, Missouri, 978-0-7643-3194-7, $14.99
Missouri Hauntings, 978-0-7643-3119-0, $14.99
Ghosts of St. Louis: The Lemp Mansion and Other Eerie Tales, 978-0-7643-2688-2

Cover photo: Lonely Wind Mill © Ronald Blekicki.
Courtesy of bigstockphoto.com.

Copyright © 2010 by Beth Cooper
*Unless otherwise noted, all photos are the property of the author.
Library of Congress Control Number: 2009938477

All rights reserved. No part of this work may be reproduced or used in any form or by any means—graphic, electronic, or mechanical, including photocopying or information storage and retrieval systems—without written permission from the publisher.

The scanning, uploading and distribution of this book or any part thereof via the Internet or via any other means without the permission of the publisher is illegal and punishable by law. Please purchase only authorized editions and do not participate in or encourage the electronic piracy of copyrighted materials.

"Schiffer," "Schiffer Publishing Ltd. & Design," and the "Design of pen and ink well" are registered trademarks of Schiffer Publishing Ltd.

Designed by "Sue"
Type set in Grasshopper/NewBskvll BT

ISBN: 978-0-7643-3390-3
Printed in the United States of America

Schiffer Books are available at special discounts for bulk purchases for sales promotions or premiums. Special editions, including personalized covers, corporate imprints, and excerpts can be created in large quantities for special needs. For more information contact the publisher:

Published by Schiffer Publishing Ltd.
4880 Lower Valley Road
Atglen, PA 19310
Phone: (610) 593-1777;
Fax: (610) 593-2002
E-mail: Info@schifferbooks.com

For the largest selection of fine reference books on this and related subjects, please visit our web site at:
www.schifferbooks.com
We are always looking for people to write books on new and related subjects. If you have an idea for a book please contact us at the above address.

This book may be purchased from the publisher.
Include $5.00 for shipping.
Please try your bookstore first.
You may write for a free catalog.

In Europe, Schiffer books are distributed by
Bushwood Books
6 Marksbury Ave.
Kew Gardens
Surrey TW9 4JF England
Phone: 44 (0) 20 8392 8585; Fax: 44 (0) 20 8392 9876
E-mail: info@bushwoodbooks.co.uk
Website: www.bushwoodbooks.co.uk

Contents

Acknowledgments

† My appreciation to my sister Cathy, who spent many hours collecting information for the ghost tours. Without her, the tours — and this book — would not have been the success they are today.

† My greatest appreciation to Devin, who stuck with me on the final edits, even though the weather was so fine outside!

† Special thanks to Janet for the Kansas City stories; her knowledge of the area is amazing, and so is her network!

† Also thanks to Chris, Doug, and Deb... the human encyclopedias that have the answer to everything in their heads. I owe you a margarita!

† Finally, to Captain Jim, leader of the Meyer-Cooper Alliance... thank you for your patience. This book is done, onward to the second!

Introduction

The Haunted History of Kansas

The history and drama of human experience in Kansas lends itself to the many hauntings found across the state. After the Kansas-Nebraska Act in 1854, settlers poured into Kansas, setting the stage for Bleeding Kansas and the Civil War. The Act established the Kansas Territory, which encompassed the plains from the Missouri border to the eastern base of the Rocky Mountains. Overnight Kansas became the battleground for balancing the congressional power shared by anti-slavery Northern states and pro-slavery Southern states. The anti-slavery North feared that slavery in Kansas would allow its extension into the West. The pro-slavery South feared that Kansas, if free, would lead to the end of slavery in the Union. For six years Kansas Territory was a battleground waged with guns and the ballot box. Not until 1861, as Southern states began to secede from the Union, was Kansas made a free state by the Northern controlled Congress.

Kansas soon became a centrally located transportation hub for westward expansion. The Oregon, Santa Fe, and California trails passed through the state, as did the Pony Express. Railroads such as the Union Pacific and the Atchison, Topeka, and Santa Fe, snaked across the plains, moving the goods necessary for a growing nation. The ghost stories featured here are based on local historical research. Without knowing the events of the past — and about the dead often tragically tied to them — there would be no understanding why we, though unsettling and sometimes terrifying, walk among so many ghosts in Kansas.

When my sister Cathy Ramirez and I started Ghost Tours of Kansas five years ago, our dream was to share the stories of our home town. Many of the tales featured in this book are drawn heavily from the Topeka tour, since it's the one we have been doing the longest and with which we have the most experience.

The tours have expanded into cities across the state. We have found that each community, with its unique history, provides a different type of tour experience. For example, Lawrence still retains a psychic energy relating to Quantrill's Raid, while Atchison has remnants of bootlegging, contraband, and prostitution. Leavenworth, meanwhile, features a military and prison heritage and Kansas City is vivid with a mixture of ethnic and Native American history.

Local historians have provided much of the background information for the tours, as well as attended investigations. Doug Wallace and Chris Meinhardt were invaluable with their knowledge of Kansas's history and the Underground Railroad. Doug joined investigators at Constitution Hall in Topeka, presenting historic facts to paranormal experiences and adding a new facet to the process of documenting paranormal activity. Chris brought the story of the Free State Capitol to life, weaving a connection between many of our tour cities.

Historian and author Deb Goodrich brought humor and detail, especially the stories relating to Lawrence, Topeka, and Leavenworth. Born in the South, Deb provided a unique perspective to local history. Her book *Stories in Stone: A sharing of the lives of some who rest in Topeka Cemetery* is used as a resource for our tour stop at Topeka Cemetery; she has also attended investigations and is a tour guide for Ghost Tours of Kansas.

We recommend the book *Bloody Dawn* by Tom Goodrich as the definitive guide to Quantrill's Raid in Lawrence, which is considered by some to be the most violent act of domestic terrorism in the United States until the Oklahoma City bombing in 1995.

Through research and investigation, the tour staff provides authentic haunted locations based on evidence and personal experiences, avoiding the traps of hearsay and urban myth. Two paranormal investigation teams have partnered with Ghost Tours of Kansas to provide documentation of spirit activity at many of our locations.

The Paranormal Encounter Documentation Research Organization (PEDRO) has provided key evidence at many of our Kansas City metro locations. Members Janet Reed, Joe Kline, and Dawanna Fangohr are not only tour guides for Ghost Tours of Kansas, but they are also active in historic community projects, including Kaw Point and Union Cemetery. Since 2004 they have investigated over one hundred locations, many of which are included in the Kansas City and Shawnee tours.

Nick Spantgos and Keith Ross of Topeka founded Paranormal Research Investigators (PRI) three years ago after Nick was impacted by a personal ghost experience. They have investigated sites across the state, most notably two of the most haunted buildings in Kansas: Constitution Hall in Topeka and Holton House in Holton. The team takes a scientific approach to each investigation and carefully documents its evidence.

Because we believe in heritage tourism and the value of historic buildings in a community, Ghost Tours of Kansas features only public buildings, with a few exceptions. It is important that tour visitors have the opportunity to go back to haunted locations and talk to the business owners, staff, and management after the tour.

We are proud to share these stories about the history and haunts of Kansas... So sit back and enjoy!

Weather and the Paranormal

"In Kansas, you know you're in trouble when the storm chasers and the ghost investigators are in your town at the same time," joked Devin Cooper, a paranormal investigator and tour guide.

In particular, an investigation in Leavenworth on April 25, 2009 proved to be somewhat challenging.

"I was really freaking out," said Andrea Isaia, a member of Paranormal Research Investigators (PRI). "We followed a tornado for about twenty miles as we traveled from Lawrence to Leavenworth. We saw houses and trees damaged. A forty-minute trip lasted nearly two hours."

During the investigation at Leavenworth's Santa Fe Depot Diner, some team members sat in the basement while the tornado sirens were sounding.

Paranormal investigators theorize that weather has an impact on ghost activity.

"There was more activity during this second investigation," explained tour guide Cathy Ramirez. "We think part of that is because of the storm and the electricity from the lightning. Spirits need energy to manifest, and lightning can provide this energy."

Other investigations may have also been impacted by weather.

"During the first investigation at the Holton Country Club, we had a rain storm," said Devin. "Before it started raining, we had a variety of activity. After the rain, the activity seemed to just stop."

There are many theories concerning the effect of weather and moon phases on paranormal activity, but the bottom line for most investigators is: "Every day is a good day for a ghost hunt."

Chapter One:
Atchison

Atchison has a reputation for being haunted. It also has a reputation as the town that had it all: liquor, prostitution, gambling, and smuggling.

Ghost Tours of Kansas realized it would be a big project to tackle the ghosts of Atchison. The city is unique from other tour cities since it was settled as a pro-slavery town in 1854 with strong ties to Missouri. Atchison offers a rich background that is fodder for ghost enthusiasts and historians, so it was a challenge to choose only the best stories for the tour.

The ghost tour team prevailed, creating a tour based on research and interviews. The tour features only authentic haunted locations. It does not include urban myths, legends, or private homes. Thus the "Brothels and Beer Halls" ghost tour of Atchison was established.

But first we share the story of Atchison's Ghost Child, believed to be the first documented haunting in Atchison. It will send chills up your spine...

Atchison's Ghost Child

Newspapers publish ghost stories, especially around Halloween when the locals are interested in area haunts. Some articles are extraordinary, such as this story published in the *Atchison Globe* on January 3, 1878.

During research for the Atchison tour, staff reviewed a news clipping that described the first documented haunting in Atchison. A man who had suffered the death of his child submitted the feature anonymously...it is very detailed and believable.

According to the article, a man, his wife, and their young child lived in one of the poorer sections of town. He described the neighborhood as "dismal and unfrequented, yet they still lived comfortably and contentedly" for six years.

Tragedy struck when the couple's daughter kissed them good-night, went upstairs to bed, and then died while sleeping.

The father struggled with his feelings. "I would not attempt to describe the great grief and humiliation of this deplorable circumstance, when nobody but us and the gravedigger followed the dear little body to the grave."

The distraught father managed his grief by delving into work, from daybreak until dusk, usually home after 7 p.m. It wasn't until later that he realized what a mistake it was to leave his wife in a dreary old house without a companion to pass the weary hours.

Months passed before he noticed his wife becoming sadder. One particular evening, she finally told him of her experiences. She explained to him that while she was brooding in her loneliness downstairs, she started to believe that her little girl was playing in the sleeping room above. Her husband felt his wife was still grief-stricken until he himself heard the sounds of his little girl Emma playing in the empty room upstairs.

At this point in the article, the man wrote, "When I say she complained of strange noises, I am afraid people will accuse me of attempting to tell a ghost story, but I hope no one will be so inconsiderate until they hear me through."

The noises of rattling dishes, moving boxes, and the sounds of childish feet pacing across the floor in search of lost treasures could be heard from upstairs while the couple was downstairs.

The man continues in the story, "At another time it seemed as if the child was rocking in her chair, and the burden of a familiar lullaby was indistinctly heard. The door would then be opened, and the feet again pattered to and from the playroom, long since shut up and heavily locked.

"On occasion just at dusk while listening with beating heart to peculiar noises the pattering feet came to the stair landing and a voice called 'Mamma! Mamma!', which was quickly recognized as that of the dead child."

"I do not know the hour, but it was late when I was disturbed by my wife rising in bed. Remembering that I had intended to keep awake, without giving evidence of it, I quietly listened… Certainly there was a pattering of feet and although I had carefully locked the door it was standing wide open. My wife called to the phantom as though it were the child in life and asked it to come to her. As certainly as I live, I heard the scrambling up on the bed and my wife informed me the next morning that if she ever embraced her child in her life, she embraced her that night."

Based on the story, the haunts continued more regularly and even outside the house. One sunny day, his wife came to his place of business, still holding the door open behind her; the husband heard the sound of a child's feet come into the room. The wife informed her husband that on the way to his work, the footsteps would stop while groups of children were playing so the mother patiently waited.

The article states, "The dainty boots of a five-year-old child distinctly walked beside her all the way to Commercial Street…the noise did not differ from that of her own shoe except lighter."

The husband explains in the article that a great many of these circumstances took place.

Another of the more notable ones was when he came home one day to find the playroom strewn with all of Emma's toys. This was highly unusual for he had secretly locked all of her toys away in a room that his wife never had knowledge of. The husband called his wife's attention to this incident and for the first time he noticed a change in his wife's manner. She gently scolded an invisible child for her carelessness and proceeded to pick up the toys.

This was the fateful day her husband decided the ghost was affecting his wife's mind. He left his growing business and their home in order to protect his wife's sanity.

The last statement expresses these words, "I give these facts to the world simply because they are curious. I cannot explain them. I will be laughed at by many, but those who have followed their hopes to an early grave, will give me sympathy, if not credence."

Now onto the Brothels and Beer Halls...

Riverhouse

After a tough week of working on the railroad or floating up and down the river, working men found that Atchison was a great place for entertainment. Who better to provide the entertainment than working girls!

"The proprietress, Ella Donoughe, paraded her girls around the building so railroad workers and steamboat patrons and employees could see the goods," explained Cathy. "She operated a booming business for quite a few years."

Originally the headquarters for the Atchison and Nebraska Railroad, the Riverhouse was constructed in 1870 on the banks of the Missouri River because of its proximity to the newly laid railroad tracks. As the business expanded, more space was needed and the headquarters moved to the Union Depot.

Ella Donoughe purchased the property at 100 Commercial Avenue in 1887 as a location for female "boarders."

"A lot of old-timers give Ella the credit for creating Atchison's reputation as a brothel and beer hall center during that time period," said Cathy. "Wealthy men as well as the working class patronized Riverhouse."

Miss Ella managed the business until 1900 and then sold it to Miss Lulu Howard, who continued operating the business as a brothel. According to Cathy, the business boomed despite Lulu being arrested and charged with maintaining a house of prostitution. "If anything, her arrests made the business more successful and well-known," she said.

William Dolan purchased the building in 1916 and turned it into a coffee factory. It was the end of an era as reputable commerce replaced prostitution in Atchison. Dolan continued to expand, eventually adding a peanut factory. He operated the business for thirty-four years.

"Supposedly you could smell the aroma of coffee and roasting peanuts for miles around," commented Cathy. "For a while there was also a candy factory...molasses can be found on the floor of the Riverhouse Restaurant."

Current owner Roy Swope was not a believer in ghosts... until his customers started reporting strange occurrences with no rational explanations for them.

The Riverhouse claims to have several haunts that have surprised both adult and children patrons.

"People were telling me they felt as though they were being watched," explained Roy. "A few told me they would hear footsteps walk to the back of their chair and stop…as though someone was standing right behind them."

The most prominent ghost in the dining area is believed to be that of an older gentleman with a mischievous nature. Said Roy, "Cell phones, dishes, and other items are knocked off the tables while customers are dining… We think it's the ghostly gentleman pulling pranks."

A ghostly woman has also made her presence known in the dining room, manifesting and then disappearing. She has also been seen on the staircase, walking heavily up and down the stairs. She really catches the attention of children.

According to Roy, "Toddlers and young children of patrons seem to communicate with the entity… While parents are paying at the register, I have seen children waving, pointing, and talking to something on the landing that only they can see. My own grandson was waving to something on the landing."

Other children hide behind their parents' legs or cried while they were looking at the landing.

During a past investigation, an investigator with a K-2 meter claimed his instrument was "going haywire" while he was standing on the landing.

Haunts are active in other areas, especially the waitress station.

"I was in the main dining area when I heard a loud crash in the waitress station," said Roy. "I ran in to make sure no one was hurt. Two scared waitresses told me the mirror on the wall didn't just fall down…it flew straight out from the wall and then crashed to the floor."

The first floor ladies' restroom is another spirited location. A waitress returning from the restroom claimed that the stall door was banging open and shut on its own accord and the water was turned on and running…yet she was the only one in the room.

Even a nine-year-old girl told Roy that he had ghosts.

"A few months after we opened a girl told me that there was a ghost of a pretty lady in the restroom," he said. "The girl also saw the same ghost in the hallway while I was giving a tour of the building to her and her mother."

The sound of heavy footsteps is the most common indication of ghost activity. Roy has investigated the building on more than one occasion, thinking someone had broken in...only to find he was alone.

Steve, a construction worker, spent time working here and was very specific about his tools, keeping the equipment tidy and in its place.

"I noticed that the tools were in disarray and thought it very strange," explains Roy. "I asked Steve what had happened, and he mentioned that he heard the sounds of dancing feet on the second level. We think the spirit also moved the tools around."

Spirits can attach to persons, places, and objects. One of the most unusual stories from the Riverhouse is also one of the most mysterious.

According to Roy, a husband and wife had dinner at the restaurant. "They returned to me later, saying they had something that belonged here...it seems they were returning a ghost," he said.

The couple believed that an entity attached to them at the restaurant. As they traveled home, they both had an uneasy feeling. Once at their apartment, they noticed strange things happening, such as moved showerheads, toilet tissue rolled onto the floor, the refrigerator door opening, and TV channels switching.

The couple returned to Riverhouse and, jokingly or not, said they were bringing back something that belonged there, and proceeded to tell Roy what had been going on.

Even skeptics can change their mind about ghosts after visiting the former brothel. A family group had dinner and a tour of the building. The oldest girl made it clear that she did not believe in ghosts, but her opinion changed when she took a photo of the exterior and captured an image of a little boy and girl looking out the upper level window. The little boy had a cowboy hat on and the little girl was wearing a prairie bonnet. All features were present except the children had no eyes...just the eye sockets. The girl ran in to tell Roy, yelling, "I believe! I believe!"

With the vivid history of the Riverhouse and its location near the Missouri River, it is easy to believe that ghosts still consider the place to be home.

Willowbrook

A charming shop near the downtown is also a haunted shop. Brett Huskamp opened Willowbrook nearly seven years ago. Originally a print shop, the building was a pool hall during the 1920s and 30s, catering to the usual types of vices.

Since opening the store, Brett has experienced numerous random haunts and said that he has noticed that remodeling and renovation increases the paranormal activity.

In October 2002, a two-year-old boy named Keegan went into the restroom. He returned very quickly, running back to the front of the store to get Brett, shouting as he ran, "Brett! Brett! There is someone in the restroom!"

He was very adamant, so Brett went back to the restroom with him and showed him that no one was there. Little Keegan pointed to the corner cabinet and said, "The woman went in there."

Willowbrook has a ghost...and some really fun shopping.

A customer made the very same claim. A woman saw a female ghostly figure disappear into the corner cabinet of the restroom. She described the woman as wearing vintage clothing. Others have had the feeling of being watched while in the restroom.

Brett told us an unusual story of a glass globe that was on display in the middle of a table. The display included a small figurine. While busy in another room, Brett heard a loud crash. He quickly walked to the table to see what had happened: the globe had been smashed to the ground and the figurine was beheaded. Nothing else on the table had been moved or knocked over.

The ghosts that reside at Willowbrook seem to be infatuated with the light fixtures. One morning Brett arrived at the shop and discovered one of the fluorescent bulbs had been taken out of the fixture on the ceiling and was lying on the floor, miraculously, unbroken.

Another light fixture sustained quite a bit of damage. Again, Brett opened the shop one morning and discovered a chandelier that had been hanging on a heavy "S" hook had shattered on the floor.

"The hook was still hanging from the ceiling," he explained. "There was no way a wind could have knocked the light down."

A ghostly voice scared two employees into being believers. They were sorting items at the front desk when they both thought that they heard footsteps. The footsteps stopped right between them and they heard a loud voice say, "Get Out!" Both ladies were petrified and, closing up, asked Brett to return to the shop.

"One of the employees was a total non-believer in ghosts," said Brett, "but after this incident she may have changed her mind."

Footsteps are a common occurrence, as well as the security alarms going off in the middle of the night.

"I have no doubt we have a haunt here at Willowbrook," concluded Brett.

Feel free to stop by the shop and ask Brett about his ghosts... perhaps your visit to the restroom will turn into a haunted experience.

Elks Lodge

What does it take for a fellow to get a drink around here? Sometimes, he needs to build his own club!

In New York City, a group of entertainers began to meet regularly as the "Jolly Corks." They held gatherings on Sundays, when blue laws prevented public joints from opening and serving alcohol. A few months after the group began meeting one of their members died, leaving his wife and children destitute.

His death encouraged the group to have a higher purpose and, on February 16, 1868, with a mission statement and a set of bylaws, the new fraternal order the Benevolent and Protective Order of Elks (BPOE) was established. Elk was chosen over buffalo as the club symbol because the elk was considered peaceful yet fleet and defends itself when threatened.

The Elks Lodge in Atchison began in 1907 with 150 members—and a few of these early brothers may still be meeting at the lodge.

The sound of tables and chairs being pushed and moved as if making their way for dancing or some big event have been experienced upstairs, as well as footsteps.

John, a long time bartender, has experienced numerous haunts, ranging from the sound of footsteps on the third floor, lights turning on and off, doors opening and closing, and general eerie feelings.

"One evening some kids were helping me close up the place, so I asked them to walk through each of the rooms and turn off the lights," explained John. "It really scared them when the lights they had just shut off came back on. They didn't like helping me much after that."

Certain members of the club will not be alone in the building. They are uncomfortable with the feeling that they are being watched; the hairs stand up on the back of their necks.

"One member told me that he heard clanging and banging noises when he was alone in the building," said John.

One paranormal incident that was witnessed by several members captured quite a bit of attention. A lock on a main door flew off and landed on the floor several feet away.

A view of the hallway at Elks Lodge... ghostly footsteps have been heard here.

"No one really knew what to make of it," said John. "We don't think the wind could have blown it...the whole lock incident was really strange."

Even after hours, it appears that former members may still be having a party of their own.

Paolucci's Restaurant

Paolucci's Family Restaurant was chosen as the ghost tour headquarters in Atchison for many reasons: excellent food, historical significance, and ghosts!

The business was established as Paolucci's Grocery in 1894, after brothers Felix and Dominic Paolucci came to Atchison from Frosolone, Italy. Dominic's wife Rosa also worked in the store while raising their four children.

In 1983, grandson Mike and his wife Margie opened Paolucci's Restaurant.

Most of the family, at one time or another, has lived upstairs in the former Old Travelers Hotel; Mike and his family have lived there for the past fifty years. As with most old hotels, tragedy struck several times, including a suicide involving a family member.

Paolucci's is the ghost tour headquarters in Atchison... It offers family dining and a few ghosts.

"My aunt committed suicide with a pistol in her room," recalled Mike. "My older brother heard the shot and another brother found the body. We were just kids when it happened… it was a grisly experience."

The second death involved a gentleman boarder. "It was about twenty-five years ago — a man had a heart attack while in the bathroom," Mike explained. "He ended up dying and was wedged behind the door. It was several hours before we could get to his body."

Later a psychic, invited to do a brief investigation of the restaurant, detected a presence in the upstairs bathroom...the same bathroom where the gentleman had died.

Stories of haunts in the building have been circulating since Mike was a small child.

"I personally remember when I was a little kid telling my parents that a ghost had taken away my truck," said Mike. "The other kids would ask our folks if they had seen the ghost. Of course, they did not know what we were talking about. I believed for a long time there was some kind of a spirit in the closet."

During remodeling, several workmen claimed that the lights would flicker or turn on and off. They also said that objects would move around.

Even restaurant and lounge patrons have commented that they had the feeling of being watched...as though a presence was close by.

There have been at least two fires while Paolucci's has been in business. The smell of smoke can generate some anxiety, so the owners are concerned when they detect that particular odor...and at random times, both Mike and Margie have detected the strong smell of ghostly smoke.

"When it happens, we do a complete search of the premises, thinking something is on fire," explained Mike. "We can't find any reason for the smoke odor."

On one occasion the restaurant was crowded when the odor occurred. The owners, concerned for the safety of their customers, searched the building for evidence of fire. None could be found. Within a matter of minutes, the smell dissipated.

The owners don't worry too much about the ghosts...*everyone* is welcome at Paolucci's!

Chapter Two:

Holton

Bold anti-slavery pioneers, escorted by General James Lane down the trail to freedom he created, arrived at Holton in 1856. The town, named after Wisconsin abolitionist E. D. Holton, was established near Banner and Elk creeks on the rolling hills of the Kansas prairie. A log fort was constructed, but the new citizens were too frightened to spend the winter in town because of raiders and Indian attacks; they spent the winter of 1856 in Topeka, returning in the spring to find the fort intact.

Holton was the northern terminus for the James Lane Trail and was instrumental in moving escaping slaves northward to freedom.

Abolitionist John Brown frequently transported runaway slaves following the James Lane Trail. During one particular trip in 1859, Brown and his men traveled from Topeka into Holton with eleven slaves he had raided from Missouri and a twelfth that was delivered along the way. They made their way from the station in Topeka, after obtaining clothes, food, and water, and continued in horse-drawn wagons with false bottoms in case the slaves needed a place to hide. The group ended up stopping at Fullers Cabin because of high waters that couldn't be crossed.

A posse made up of men from Atchison, under the leadership of John P. Wood, a deputy United States marshal from Lecompton, were notified of Brown's arrival at Holton. But the posse was afraid to attack and Wood, despite outnumbering Brown, sent for reinforcements. The Brown Party decided to go ahead and cross the waters even though the posse was ready and waiting. Amazingly, the posse members mounted their horses and departed, with only four men remaining to prove their bravery. This event in history received the name Battle of the Spurs, since spurs were the only weapons used as the posse fled on horseback. No shots were ever fired.

Other well-known historic figures who lived in Holton include prohibitionist Carrie Nation and Buffalo Bill Cody, the latter was an express rider after the war.

Today, Holton is a prosperous community with a charming town square and residents who are proud of their agricultural heritage.

Holton House

For PRI investigator Nick Spantgos, it was easy to choose Holton House, a former mortuary, as the most haunted building in Kansas. The deciding factor was the thermal image recording.

"We were running a FLIR thermal sweep when we saw a profile on the screen walk through a closed door," explains Nick. "It was the most amazing thing I have ever seen."

That evidence, along with personal experiences and EVP (Electronic Voice Phenomenon) recordings, made the Holton House a hit with investigators.

The Holton House has a long history in the area. Granville King, a Missouri businessman, built the house in 1888. His family resided there in comfortable luxury until 1930, when the building was purchased by Porterfield Funeral Home and continued to be a funeral parlor with several owners over the next thirty years. During that time, the house underwent many renovations, from a residential dwelling, to funeral parlor, to apartments, and now a bed and breakfast.

Many of the remarkable architectural structures remain from the time of construction. A massive truss system on the third floor provided support for the structure. During the Victorian era, most homes were large, but built with many small rooms. The Holton House is unique, with the main level of the house built with an open living area where wakes and funeral services were eventually held. A large porch protected farmers as they gazed through the front window, viewing the body and paying their respects, without having to dress up and come inside. Another unusual feature that remains is a casket-sized elevator located near the kitchen, dropping into the embalming room down in the basement.

Current owners Shaun and Tara Deegan have experienced ghostly activity at their inn.

"After we purchased the building and started renovations, it was not unusual to see shadow figures and hear women's voices while I was working on different projects," said Shaun.

He sometimes worked late into the evening, with the early morning hours being the prime time for the ghosts. While working in the Shea Room, Shaun thought his wife had entered

In this bay window, bodies used to be displayed for the farmers so the visitors would not track dirt throughout the business.

the room. "I saw a woman's figure in the room, but kept on working, thinking it was Tara," he explained. "When I called her name, there was no response." He checked the room and realized that no one else was there. It became a normal occurrence after that to hear female voices as he worked alone in the building.

The Shea Room seems to be the most active room at Holton House, as Shaun recalled another experience he had in the room: "I was sound asleep, and awakened from a deep sleep to the sound of very loud [female] voices in the dining room. It was 2 a.m. I was alone in the house... by then I decided to go home!"

In this former mortuary, the Shea Suite is a room where lights go on and off and voices have been heard.

The Shea Room and the dining room are directly above the embalming area in the basement... Tara has also experienced unusual activity in that vicinity.

"It is not unusual to find chairs that were pushed into the dining tables pulled back out," she said. "At the time I thought the children did it, but I now realize that spirits may have been involved."

Holton House has a steady group of overnight visitors as well as long-term guests. When there is a shortage of nurses at the Holton Hospital, Shaun and Tara often provide lodging for nurses on call. Said Shaun, "One nurse checked in for the evening and was checking out a few hours later. She didn't like the ghostly presence that she found in her room."

According to Nick, PRI recorded a male voice saying his name was Justin in the Shea Room. "Several of us were in the room at the time, and none of us were named Justin," he said. "This was more evidence of the haunting."

While in the attic, investigators discovered the presence of a boy named Patrick.

According to Cathy Ramirez, co-owner of Ghost Tours of Kansas, "I asked the question, 'what is your name,' and on our digital recorder a clear voice said 'Patrick'. Another EVP by the child was that of a choice cuss word, which made us laugh after we reviewed the tapes."

People driving by Holton House have actually made the claim that they could see a child's face looking out the attic window. Perhaps this was Patrick, watching the busy street scene below.

During the first investigation at Holton House, Nick and investigator Keith Ross saw a shadow figure pass through the kitchen hallway; they moved towards the area in hopes of capturing the entity on film, but were unsuccessful. The incident corroborates Shaun's personal experiences of seeing figures or shadows in that portion of the house.

The elevator is another area of paranormal activity. An EVP captured during an investigation was a voice saying "Help me" ... though no one had been in the elevator at any point during the investigation.

"We never asked any questions in that area," explained Cathy. "The recorder was deliberately left there and had picked up the voice saying 'help me.'"

Shaun and Tara agree that the inn is haunted, but it does not seem to bother the patrons too much. "Our chicken dinners are popular in town," said Shaun. "Maybe that is why the ghosts are here… to enjoy a good meal and a nice place to spend the night."

Small Town Hanging

Quiet towns like Holton have their share of unfortunate deeds. One of the most violent occurred in 1899 with a murder and subsequent lynching of a young man named Henry Sanderson.

It was on a Sunday afternoon when Henry paid a visit to the Fleisher property to present his intentions to sixteen-year-old Myrtle Fleisher. She and other family members were standing in the yard chatting when Henry arrived.

The young lady did not favorably receive Henry's intentions, and her rebuff made him angry. He pulled out a rifle and started shooting. The first shot hit her aunt, Mrs. John Fleisher, in the abdomen. The nature of her wound killed her immediately. Several more shots were fired at the group, missing Myrtle, as everyone ran for cover. Henry decided to make an escape towards the town of Mayetta.

As he raced ahead of the law, Henry tried to reload his gun with painful results. While loading, a shell became lodged in the chamber. He struck the butt of the gun against the ground, causing the gun to discharge. The bullet struck his arm, totally shattering the bone.

Shortly after reaching Mayetta, Henry was captured and taken to Horr's Restaurant on the south side of the Holton Town Square. Threats were made and gossip was flying, but oddly, the sheriff was unconcerned about mob or vigilante activity. By 2 a.m., a party of twenty-five men stealthily moved down the alley behind the restaurant and captured Henry.

Henry struggled with his captors, but his injury and the will of the mob made resistance futile. At the high bridge crossing Banner Creek the men tied the rope to a rail, placed the noose around Henry's neck, and dropped him six feet over the bridge. Fate was not kind, as his neck did not break;

rather, he slowly strangled to a painful death. The sheriff and his men found Henry's body about two hours later. His body, with the noose still wrapped around his neck, was placed on display for the local citizens to view from early morning until late afternoon. No one was punished for the lynching, but the identities of the mob members were known throughout the county.

Ghosts have been seen on bridges, and Banner Creek Bridge is no exception. Old-timers recall rumors of a ghost, perhaps that of Henry, on the lips of schoolchildren for years after the hanging.

Hotel Josephine

Hotel Josephine is one of the oldest, continually operating hotels in Kansas. A. D. Walker built the structure in 1889, naming it after his daughter. Throughout its existence, some very famous people spent time there, including President Grover Cleveland, Carrie Nation, Charles Curtis, and actress Kirstie Alley.

Over the years, Hotel Josephine has been the epitome of hospitality. Fourteen passenger trains made stops at the nearby depot, directing passengers to the comforts and luxury of the hotel. Many a horse and buggy were parked in front of the hotel while patrons enjoyed the social events inside. Some of the original furnishings, including Josephine Walker's graduation portrait and piano, still embellish the rooms.

And ghost stories have been attached to the hotel for a long time.

"Hotels in general seem to have ghosts because of the amount of human activity," explained Cathy.

However, according to historic research done by Ghost Tours of Kansas, there are no documented suicides or murders associated with Hotel Josephine.

"Perhaps the ghosts that linger are reliving the enjoyable experiences of their past," Cathy suggested.

During deer and pheasant season, hunters spent their days in the fields and their nights at the hotel. Sleep may not have been easy...

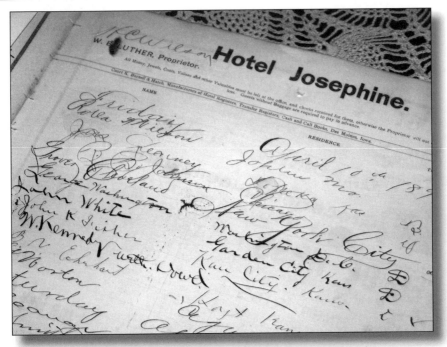

This is the guest book showing the numerous people who have visited this historic part of Holton. If you look close enough, you'll see Grover Cleveland's name.

† "A few years ago hunters staying in the corner room upstairs witnessed a picture that started spinning in circles on the wall," explained Cathy. "They were scared enough from the experience that they requested a different room."

† A patron temporarily living in one of the rooms on the top floor claimed that "his bed would rock so much, it would wake him up." He also reported hearing strange noises.

† A recent guest saw strange lights floating above the door and felt a presence sitting in the rocking chair. She asked to move downstairs to another room the next morning.

† Guests will often complain that their bed is uncomfortable because they are unable to sleep on one side...it's as though an entity of some kind was occupying the other half.

Some of the many beautiful and original pieces are still used in the hotel. Perhaps the spirits are comfortable here because of the familiar surroundings.

Employees have no doubt there are ghosts in the building, and the hotel is becoming a popular place for weekend ghost enthusiasts to spend the night. During an investigation several years ago, the manager described some of her experiences.

"My experiences happen mostly in the basement laundry room... the washing machine would turn off and on and the dryer door would open and close," she said.

Paranormal Research Investigators did an investigation at Hotel Josephine and acquired evidence of paranormal activity. Four different EVPs were collected, including a voice saying, "Help me!", and when asked "What is your name?", the response was "Rose Marie."

In an upstairs room, Nick recorded a brief conversation. "I felt my hair being tugged, then later on the recorder there was a male voice saying, 'Who are you? You're not supposed to be here,'" he said. "It was certainly an interesting experience!"

Evidence of spirit activity was also documented in the basement. "The mini video cam recorded whispering sounds next to an antique rocking chair," explained Nick. "It also captured the K-2 meter flashing on the chair. That was the only location in the building where the K-2 meter picked up readings."

One customer, Jim Meyer, enjoys staying at the hotel. "Where else can you spend a night with a ghost and then have a good breakfast in the morning!"

Holton Country Club

During the Great Depression, Bruce Saunders constructed the Holton Country Club as a gathering place for the local elite. In 1935, at a time when most families were struggling to put food on the table, Bruce was designing a 9-hole golf course on the property and hosting elegant private parties. During his travels, Bruce collected rocks that represented the exotic locations he had visited. The sparkling geodes, multi-colored stones, and even petrified tortoise shells embellished the fireplace, enhancing the beauty of the main room.

Tragedy struck years later when Mr. Saunders was killed while collecting his mail.

The fireplace in the ballroom of the Holton Country Club is made of rocks and crystals from all over the world and even includes two turtle shells.

"According to accounts, Saunders stepped out into the street to greet a passing friend," said Cathy. "He did not see the car coming from the other direction and was struck and killed instantly."

After Saunders' death, a restaurant opened on the main level while the owners and caretaker lived in the second floor attic.

The location re-opened as a country club in 2003...with the added bonus of a haunting.

"I have no doubt that the bar area and the main floor are haunted," said Megan Ray, the manager. "We constantly hear noises and odd activity taking place in those rooms."

What started out as a joke may have eventually become a *real* ghost.

"One night the lights went off in the bar during a snow storm," recalled Megan. "We freaked out when only half the lights went out while the others were really dim. For a while we started cracking jokes about it being the ghost from upstairs. It was less funny when the cash register went off."

Megan had jokingly asked the ghost to ring up the tab; seconds later the cash register was ringing up the beer on its own. Then, the power went out completely.

"We checked the breaker box and everything seemed normal," said Megan. "Eventually we became used to having a ghost at the bar."

Investigations have revealed a significant amount of paranormal activity at the club.

"The knob on the staircase door in the attic area began rattling and jiggling within twenty minutes of our first investigation," recalled Nick. "No one was on the other side of the door, and we could not explain why the knob was rattling that way."

Later on in the investigation, Nick watched as a bright ball of light appeared in the closet.

"It was about the size of a grapefruit... it showed for a few seconds, then disappeared," he said. "Within a few minutes an EVP was recorded saying in a very loud male voice 'That's me'."

Nick and fellow investigator Devin Cooper tried to recreate the light with flashlights, but could not duplicate the incident.

"We heard numerous disembodied voices trying to interact with us," said Devin. "My personal experience was hearing a man's voice say, 'Hey!' I looked at Nick, but he was quiet the entire time. Later, when we reviewed the evidence, it was on the recorder, along with the same voice asking for help."

During EVP work, Nick asked the spirits if they liked the investigation team visiting them. The spirit replied 'yes' as a disembodied voice that was also recorded on audio.

The Holton Country Club is one of the top five most haunted places in Kansas. The club is a spirited location... *for cocktails and ghosts*!

Holton Business District

"For us the best way to collect ghost stories is to go door-to-door and ask business owners if they have a ghost," said tour guide Andrea Isaia. "When we first began, we were surprised at the number of businesses in all of our tour cities that had ghost activity."

103 West Fourth Street
Owners of this building have frequently seen a ghostly man wearing a plaid shirt and ball cap — he briefly appears and then fades away. Prior to being a coffee shop, this location originally was a mortuary. It was one of several in the downtown area, including the Roepke building, which also housed a furniture store, and the Schillinger building.

"Undertaking was a profitable business in those days, so shops were set up all over town," explained Andrea. "It was not until 1911 that licenses were required to be an undertaker."

Expressions
This floral shop seems to be haunted by a ghost that spends time on the second floor. Besides hearing footsteps pacing back and forth, staff also hears the lock on the staircase door randomly click, as ghostly footsteps proceed down the steps. The noise dissipates as the footsteps reach the bottom.

"Since this haunting activity takes place on a regular basis in the same location, it is considered to be residual by ghost researchers," said Andrea, explaining, "The spirit is repeating the same motion over and over, and is not trying to communicate or interact with the living."

Begin Again Store

The most common haunts — objects being moved, footsteps, and hearing voices — have been reported to occur at this shop.

"Sometimes if the weather is bad for traveling home, the owner spends the night at the store," said Andrea. "You can imagine how unnerving it would be to hear footsteps pacing back and forth or voices in the basement. It is very hard to talk yourself into thinking there are people out in a storm just standing on the sidewalk talking at 3 in the morning."

*Author's note: Although not haunted, these next two downtown locations are included in the tour because of their amusing historic backgrounds.

325 Hicks Joint

Carrie Nation, the saloon smasher, lived in Holton for several years with her husband, who preached at the Baptist church. It was convenient for her to march around town square with her followers, tearing up the local watering holes.

"One particular incident was at Hicks Joint," explained Andrea. "Carrie, with her hatchet and one hundred followers, went on a rampage. In Mr. Hicks's words, 'booze flowed as freely down the gutter as ditch water and in minutes my joint was a wreck.'"

New York Street

In the late 1800s, the town square was strongly divided by politics. The Democrats and their businesses were located on the south side, the Republicans on the north. Flags representing their party were posted in front of their locations; by morning the flags on both sides were usually destroyed. Eventually, the parties no longer put up their flags.

Kansas Avenue Haunts

Several houses along Kansas Avenue seem to have a ghost or two inhabiting the home. With a few exceptions, Ghost Tours of Kansas does not include private homes in order to protect the privacy of the homeowners. However, there have been times when homeowners have contacted us about paranormal activity in their home.

Haunted Toys

"A family here in Holton contacted us via email regarding their young son seeing quite an assortment of what they believed were ghosts," explained Andrea, adding, "Some of them seemed menacing."

The email, later confirmed in an interview, mentioned the child having a detailed description of several entities in the house. One that we considered to be particularly menacing was described by the child as "the witch." The child easily described exactly what the witch looked like down to the shoes. The child also held conversations with the entity. This was a clue that the family needed the help of the investigation team to see what could be done.

The same day the email arrived, Paranormal Research Investigators went over to their house for a pre-investigation interview and walkthrough of the house. After doing a thorough interview with the family, the team began scanning the entire home with EMF detectors and noticed a very high reading among several of the child's toys; in particular, an electronic piano gave off a reading of well over 200-mg from three feet away.

"The piano, along with several other devices in the room, caused what paranormal investigators call a fear cage," said Nick. "High EMF fields can cause many different symptoms to an individual such as paranoia, fatigue, skin irritation, and even auditory and visual hallucinations. This child was constantly exposed to a very high EMF, causing these symptoms in the child."

PRI recommended to the family that they needed to unplug the devices when they were not in use to see if the child's experiences went away.

"PRI likes to investigate as a last resort," adds tech manager Ben Nichols. "One month later PRI received a thank you letter from the family explaining how since they followed PRI advice the child had not experienced any paranormal activity. The family was relieved that there weren't ghosts in the house."

The Ghost Children

Ghostly children started appearing at one home on the block two years ago.

"I have lived here for over twenty years, and did not have any ghosts until recently," said the owner. "They are dressed in Victorian style clothing and are ages 6 to 12."

The ghosts may appear every day or go several months without appearing. The owner believes that her own energy might be attracting the ghost children.

"I have worked with children most of my life, and I have some psychic ability," she explained. "Perhaps the children come to me looking for help, comfort, and attention? It is an answer we may never know."

Children have manifested themselves in front of the owner in several rooms of the house. A child appeared next to the TV while the owner was sitting on the divan, but the incident that made the owner uneasy was when a boy appeared between the sofa and the coffee table; he had a mischievous grin on his face that sent chills up the owners' spine. The owner was lying on the sofa and the ghost boy was staring right at her. "Usually, all the children stare through me, or away from me, no matter what room I am in," she said.

A child also appeared between the bed and the window while the homeowner was upstairs.

The resident of the home is not fearful of the haunted environment. What makes this location unusual is the fact that historic research does not explain why children would haunt the house and only in the last two years. Also, it is odd that the resident does not see the same child twice.

"The house does not exhibit the standard paranormal activity, such as noises, lights flickering, or footsteps," noted Andrea. "We do know the previous owner died in the home, but we do not believe she is haunting the home."

It is an interesting mystery!

Chapter Three:

Kansas City

At the confluence of the Kansas and Missouri rivers is a vibrant and culturally diverse city that is rich in history and haunts. Ghost investigators theorize that the rivers enhance the paranormal activity in the "most haunted city in Kansas."

With the passage in 1854 of the Kansas-Nebraska Act, which left the question of slavery to the people, Eastern settlers moved onto lands formerly occupied by the Wyandot tribe along the Kansas River and dubbed their fledgling town Wyandot City.

The conflict over slavery made the border a dangerous place for free-state pioneers. Fleeing slaves and border ruffians were drawn to Wyandot City because of its proximity to Missouri.

Kansas City was incorporated in 1884 and became a prosperous city with major industries that included railroads, meat packing plants, and stockyards. Immigrants from Croatia and Slovenia arrived as workers for the booming new economy, turning Kansas City into the center of industry in the area. Floods impacted the development of the community, with major flooding occurring in 1903, 1951, and 1993.

Today, Kansas City features beautiful period architecture and a heritage of undaunted citizens.

Kaw Point

Kaw Point, located at the confluence of the Missouri and Kansas rivers, has long been an important crossing for travelers moving towards the western prairies, including Native Americans, French traders, escaping slaves, and westward pioneers. Called "River Jordan" by escaped slaves, they returned to bathe their babies in the Kaw as a symbol of freedom.

Kaw Point was the site of the first court martial west of the Mississippi. Lewis and Clark camped for four days at the Point in 1804. During camp, two men, Privates Hugh Hall and John Collins, indulged in more than their share of the rationed rum during night watch, becoming inebriated. Both men were court marshalled and whipped for their deed. Punishment was fifty lashes for Collins and one hundred for Hall. Groaning in pain, they were at the oars the next day, continuing the voyage west on the Missouri.

Early on, boats — from small craft to steam-powered vessels — moved up and down the Kaw River transporting goods and settlers.

Later, Harry Darby, Jr. organized the Darby Corporation in the lowlands around Kaw Point in 1938, thus establishing the largest steel plate manufacturer in the nation. During World War II, Darby built Land Craft Mechanized (LCM) vehicles, producing one per day. Nearly 1,400 were launched and floated to New Orleans for the war effort.

Drowning and heart attack victims are a few of the haunts that may linger at Kaw Point, as the old bridge, now a walking trail that spans the Kaw River near the confluence, is known for jumpers; people who have lost hope find morbid solace in the liquid depths of the river.

"This is the bridge where jumpers commit suicide," explained Dawanna Gangohr, a tour guide and paranormal investigator. "Since the railroad bridge was constructed, people have chosen to end their lives by drowning in the Kaw River."

Captain Catfish is a river guide who hosts fishing parties up and down the Kaw and Missouri rivers. He points out that bodies of jumpers are rarely found.

The jumper bridge at Kaw Point is located at the confluence of the Kansas and Missouri rivers.

"Most of the time they are caught up by the current into snags or deep pools," the captain explained. "Catfish aren't real choosy about what they eat."

Other deaths have also occurred at Kaw Point.

Said Dawanna, "An elderly man who had been squatting for years on the property was required to remove his belongings. During the move, he died of a heart attack."

The most likely ghost, reported by both fishermen and investigators, is that of Lyda Conley. One of the locally famous Conley sisters, she did laundry at the confluence and has been seen making her ghostly trek to the river.

Spiritualists, pagans, and Native Americans frequently hold rituals at Kaw Point, drawn to the mystery of the water and the heritage of the location.

Fat Matt's Vortex Bar

Fat Matt is a big yellow cat.

"Yes, we figure he is the reincarnated former owner," said Joni, the current owner of Fat Matt's Vortex. "Fat Matt really likes it here!"

This former mortuary is now Fat Matt's Vortex. Shown is the basement cooling chamber used at the mortuary.

Fat Matt's Vortex Bar is a popular watering hole for locals and visitors, serving up a beer and a special Witch's Brew Cocktail that some say makes it easier to see the ghost. Employees have seen an apparition hunched over in a booth with a gun in its lap.

"The story is that a few years back the son of a former owner committed suicide at the back of the bar," said Joni.

Before the location was a bar, it was a mortuary and funeral home.

In 1922, John Stine opened a mortuary that later become Skradski Funeral Home in the early 1930s. The crematorium oven and refrigeration unit, where bodies were kept before the embalming, are still in the basement.

Nick and Keith spent time in the basement searching for paranormal activity.

"We had several EVP recordings while we were near the crematory," said Nick. "We kept hearing the faint sound of singing. I asked the spirit if it was singing, and the EVP reply was 'maybe.'"

Fat Matt's is the ghost tour headquarters for Kansas City where folks can enjoy spirits of all types.

Sauer Castle

The majestic building on the wooded hill above the river has a tragic and mysterious history.

"Curses, suicide, and treasures are part of the mystery here at Sauer Castle," noted tour guide Janet Reed. "All of which are stories that have been passed along for several generations."

The property was near the old spring where the Shawnee Indians collected water. Indian Tom Bigknife held title to the property until 1861 and then sold it.

"Folks turned that into a legend, that the land was sacred and had been stolen from Tom Bigknife," explained Janet. "The reality is there are papers at the courthouse indicating he owned, and then sold, the property."

German immigrant Anton Sauer constructed the mansion in 1871. As a prosperous businessman with seven children, he needed a home that was spacious but also indicated his social status. His wife Mary decorated the home with elegant furnishings and artwork. Although not a castle in the European sense, the style and grandeur of the place encouraged the locals to call it Sauer Castle.

The family lived comfortably in their home until tragedy struck in 1879.

Baby Helena, age fourteen months, died of illness July 15, and just a month later, on August 16, Anton died of tuberculosis in the second floor master bedroom. Both father and daughter were buried at Union Cemetery in Kansas City, Missouri.

His widow managed the estate successfully until her death in 1919.

"In order to finance the education of her daughters, Mary Sauer began selling off many of the art pieces and furnishings from the house," explained Janet. "This, along with the fact that there was a wine cellar that stored food and goods, led to speculation of buried treasure."

The only suicide in the home took place May 20, 1930 when John Perkins, husband of Sauer daughter Eva Marie, took his life with a handgun in the home. Many believe that failing health was the reason for his suicide.

The drowning of a toddler — Eva Marie's granddaughter — occurred in the swimming pool on the property a few years later.

After Eva Marie died in 1955, Paul Berry purchased the property. He lived there until his death in 1986 and was constantly dealing with trespassers and vandals, along with thrill seekers looking for ghosts.

"The ghost stories began in the 1930s and continue even now," noted Janet. "After the suicide of John Perkins and the death of the toddler, people began to think that the place was haunted."

The most popular ghost story is that of a woman seen walking on the widow's walk. Wearing a dark gown, she slowly moves back and forth as if in deep thought... Perhaps the same woman also lingers inside the tower of the mansion.

Season Ferrell, a visitor to the building several years ago, recounts her personal experience with the ghost lady in the castle:

"We had spent the whole afternoon exploring the old wine cellar and back line of the property and were walking back up the hill toward the door of the new addition of the castle when my mom, my little brothers, and I looked up at the back window of the tower," Season recalled. "Someone pointed and said, 'Do you see that?' We all looked. I vividly remember what I saw in that window...a small statured woman with long dark hair and dark eyes that were looking out onto the hill in horror as if she was observing something terrible from her favorite spot there in the tower and in her helpless position could do nothing more than watch with her hands pressed against the glass...I immediately felt her pain and began to cry... but I don't know what she was looking at."

For a while the castle was protected by a caretaker with a big dog and a "shotgun full of rock salt."

The property is listed on both the Register of Historic Kansas Places and the National Register of Historic Places. It's also a Kansas City, Kansas, Historic Landmark.

Louisa M. Alcott School

Its playground now a parking lot, the L. M. Alcott School was a bustling place for an increasing number of children to learn new ideas. Built in 1922, it was styled to be more modern and open than those of the Victorian past. The school was built in stages to accommodate the growing community.

It serviced the area in a variety of ways other than education. During the Great Depression, the PTA mended and distributed clothing to local children and established a thrift shop. The school also served as a shelter in 1951 for flood victims during the rising of the Kansas River. Dikes broke in the middle of the night, with many people escaping from the flooding with nothing more than the clothing on their backs; 131 people called the school home after the flood until the school opened for the school year on September 19.

The building served as a school until 1977 and then was used for administrative personnel. The building changed purposes again in 1986, turning into the L. M. Alcott High School, an alternative school for at-risk teens; this school lasted until 1999, when it was sold for use as an arts center.

Paranormal activity is part of a typical day at the Alcott Arts Center. Directors Chris and Chuck Green describe the ghosts as being "warm and not threatening...the entire building feels very nostalgic."

The most active location seems to be the theater area. Staff members claim they have heard the laughter of a teenage boy and doors slamming during rehearsals. In the prop room, items have moved around while disconnected phones have been known to ring on occasion.

Board members have also experienced the paranormal activity.

"The boys' playroom is now the board room," explained Janet. "During meetings people have commented on a feeling of having their knees squeezed, or being pinched."

The spirit of a former janitor may also linger in the parking lot. He is most often seen while people are backing their cars. When looking in their rearview mirror, drivers see a man wearing overalls standing directly behind them; after slamming on their brakes, the apparition disappears.

The ghost of a little girl, named Sarah, also dwells in the building. She is an active spirit who has been seen in the costume room, dance rehearsal room, and the recording studio, which was formerly the girls' playroom. The most conclusive evidence of her presence took place after volunteers scraped the ceiling and walls in preparation of repainting. The following day small footsteps were found amid the dust and paint chips on the floor.

"The most startling fact about the footsteps was that they were in the middle of the floor," said Janet. "Although the building had been locked up for the evening, there were these tracks across the floor, without any explanation."

As a fundraiser, ghost investigators were invited to document the paranormal activity. Many investigative teams have visited the center — and none went away disappointed. Several groups recorded EVPs, including the voice of a little girl singing in the studio.

While this building is now a safe haven for the arts, a few ghostly specters still call it home.

Wyandotte High School

Wyandotte High School is a grand building similar in design to an European palace, but before the school was built the lot was used as a training ground for soldiers during the war. Later the lot was used as a golf course. The building was completed in March 1937, an amazing feat since construction took place during the height of the Great Depression. Funded as part of the Work Projects Administration, the cost of the school was about $2.5 million dollars and was the largest high school in the Midwest at the time.

The architecture of Wyandotte High School identifies the building as a Kansas City landmark. Towers flank the main entryway, with the west tower representing knowledge and the east representing character. According to former principal J. F. Wellemeyer, "The west was a land of pioneers, eager and ambitious to achieve and acquire, and they were true pioneers in arts and sciences as well as many newer branches of learning. The east suggests maturity, stability of character, refinement, culture, and inspiration." All appropriate sentiments for youthful development.

The interior decorations feature huge fireplaces, artwork, and trim throughout the building. The theater is exceptional in its design, seating over 1,700 guests and featuring art panels and recessed lighting. During construction of the theater, four men were killed when the ceiling collapsed; their deaths are commemorated by panels flanking each side of the stage. Students believe the ghosts of the workers may be haunting the theater.

"I was in the school production of 'The Wiz' in 2003. During a rehearsal, two girls were operating the spotlights when one of them felt something touch her," said Joe, an alumnus of the school. "The other girl saw an apparition at about the same time. Both girls were so frightened that they refused to work the spotlights anymore."

Notable stage alumni of the school include actor Ed Asner, whose signature can still be seen on the wall behind the stage, and actress Dee Wallace Stone, known for her roles in "E.T." and "The Hills Have Eyes."

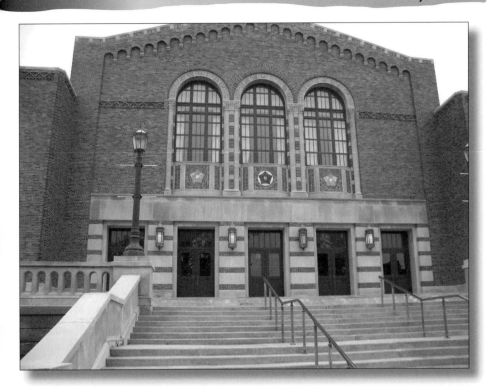

Wyandotte High School theatre is home to a ghost. Among its famous alumni is actor Ed Asner, whose signature adorns the wall behind the stage.

The janitorial staff has also experienced paranormal activity on the second floor. While working in the evenings, they have heard footsteps in the hallways and doors slamming for no apparent reason.

A legacy of education and pride, plus plenty school spirit, remains at Wyandotte High School.

Memorial Hall, Kansas City

"I Fall to Pieces" might be classic Patsy Cline, but it also foreshadowed her death in an airplane crash on March 5, 1963. Fans of Patsy Cline believe her spirit lingers at the location where she performed her final concert, giving encores for an appreciative crowd.

Memorial Hall was constructed to commemorate over 6,400 young men of Wyandotte County who served their country during the Great War. Businessman Harry Darby petitioned

Memorial Hall in Kansas City is where singer Patsy Cline made her last performance before her untimely death.

the city to approve $500,000 in bonds to build the hall and groundbreaking ceremonies took place May 14, 1923. The building features an auditorium with seating for 3,500, meeting rooms for veterans groups, and a chapel turned ballroom that seats six hundred on the third floor.

The ballroom is one area of the building that seems to have paranormal activity.

"When I am upstairs, I feel as though I am being watched," explained the evening manager. "I have heard footsteps, even though I am the only person in the building."

There is also is a haunting in the stage area. During a concert, a man working on the lights was electrocuted and fell to his death during the performance. But he may not be the only one haunting the area.

According to Janet, "A few years ago a roadie for a rock band died backstage...People believe his ghost might still be hanging out backstage."

And, in the silence, the unforgettable Patsy Cline soulfully performs her ghostly encore....

Huron Cemetery

Visitors made a surprising discovery during a ghost tour in the fall of 2008.

"Our group was walking around the cemetery, taking photos, asking questions, and enjoying the thrill of being in a spooky location," said Janet, "when a tour participant came up to me with an amazing photo of a large streak of light hovering above the grave of Helena Conley."

Janet believes *it* was definitely paranormal.

"Cursed be the villain that molest their grave" marks the stone commemorating Helena Conley, one of several sisters buried in Huron Cemetery. Established in 1843 after an outbreak of disease killed over fifty Wyandot tribe members, this downtown cemetery remains controversial.

According to Janet, the land is prime downtown real estate and developers have wanted to build on the property since the early 1900s. Three sisters — Lyda (birth name Eliza), Lena (birth name Helena), and Ida — took action to protect the cemetery...the burial place of their parents and family members. In order to prevent the sale, Lyda, a noted attorney, filed a permanent injunction against the Secretary of the Interior. The ladies also constructed a small wooden shack, dubbed "Fort Conley," and settled in for the "Seven Year's War" in order to protect the property.

"Lyda and Lena were passionate about saving the cemetery from land speculators," noted Janet. "They posted no trespassing signs, and guarded the place with an old shotgun."

An October 25, 1906 quote from Lyda Conley in the *Kansas City Star* newspaper states: "In this cemetery are buried one hundred of our ancestors...why should we not be proud of our ancestors and protect their graves? We shall do it, and woe be to the man that first attempts to steal a body. We are part owners of the ground and have the right under the law to keep off trespassers, the same right a man has to shoot a burglar who enters his home."

Lyda made history as the first Native American woman to present a case before the Supreme Court; the court upheld the earlier congressional act.

Huron Cemetery is a quiet part of downtown Kansas City and possibly some spirits guarding over the graves.

In 1913, Senator Charles Curtis of Topeka, who later became the only Native American Vice President of the United States, assisted the sisters in preserving the property. Congress repealed the bill authorizing the sale, but the dispute between those wanting to preserve the cemetery and those wanting to develop the land continues to this day. Even the placing of the Huron Indian Cemetery on the National Register of Historic Places in 1971 didn't stop those wanting to exploit the land.

Lyda spent her life in poverty. As an attorney, she would only take on cases of other Indians and she often did not charge for her services. Her death at age seventy-two was brutal and shocking.

Lyda was a frequent visitor to the old Carnegie Library, both to stay warm and to read. While she was walking home on the evening of May 28, 1946, a man jumped out of the bushes, hit her over the head with a brick, and stole her purse. Bystanders carried her home, where she died around 6 a.m. How much did her death cost? Twenty cents was all that she carried in her purse.

During her life Lyda was a creature of habit; in death, her ghost has been seen traversing the same route, including Kaw Point, the library, and along Third Street as she made her way home.

"It is not unusual to see the ghostly Lyda roaming the cemetery," said Janet, adding, "Doesn't it make sense that her spirit remains in the place that meant so much to her?"

Lena, while perhaps not as famous as her sister, was known for the curses she placed on those who bothered the cemetery. She liked to point out that when her house was sold for taxes in 1951 she cursed the city. Of course, that was the year of the great flood. She also took credit for the deaths of President Theodore Roosevelt's sons during war. After all, she cursed him after he signed the legislation to sell Huron Cemetery. And the untimely death of Senator Plumb, who introduced the legislation to sell the cemetery, was because of a curse.

She died in September 1958 at the age of ninety-four. It is her gravestone that warns of the harm that might befall "villains."

Many believe that the ghosts of Lena and Lyda are a protective force, wafting between the stones as they watch for threats against their precious resting place. But *another* ghost has also been seen at the cemetery, this one of a male figure standing as though on guard next to the grave of his wife and baby.

"As we stood on the sidewalk, several of us saw a shadow figure of a man, arms crossed, standing next to the grave marked 'Barnes'," said Janet. "Perhaps it was his wife and baby who were buried together after they died in childbirth."

This quiet, peaceful space downtown provides nearby residents and workers a small place to relax and possibly experience the history and spirit of former citizens.

Strawberry Hill Museum

It's not often that a ghost collects money from tourists, but that's exactly what appears to have happened at the Strawberry Hill Museum.

According to a museum volunteer, "I was on duty, guiding tours through the museum. It was a quiet afternoon, so I was surprised when I saw a small group of people in the front room, enjoying the beautiful furnishings and art. I told them they needed to go back to the entry way and purchase a ticket."

But the group already had their tickets! The volunteer was concerned, being the only one on duty.

"Who sold you the tickets?" he asked, to which the group replied, "Oh, the nice lady in the red dress!"

The Lady in Red is one of several ghosts at the museum, though board members are adamant there are no ghosts.

According to a board representative, "We don't want the reputation of being haunted and we don't want people coming here in order to see ghosts."

So while the official stance is "there are no ghosts," volunteers and guests have experienced the paranormal at Strawberry Hill Museum.

The Victorian style mansion was constructed for John and Margaret Scroggs in 1887 and was considered to be one of the finest homes in Kansas City. The family lived there until Margaret's death in 1915, when the house then passed to daughter Emma. The house was sold in 1919 to become St. John's Orphanage. Through the years additions were made to the building, so that by 1940 the orphanage was licensed to care for seventy children. The home was closed and sold in 1988 to create the museum.

The orphanage nuns were the first to report seeing the Lady in Red.

Many people have speculated that the Lady in Red is Emma, a very beautiful and flamboyant woman who loved art, culture, and the fashionable clothing of her time.

But other ghosts have also been seen in the museum, including a ghostly little girl walking around the playground and the shadow figures of nuns in the hallways.

Strawberry Hill Museum… home of the ghostly Lady in Red.

One of the more dramatic paranormal experiences happened to the catering staff before an event.

"The caterers were caught up on their tasks, so they spent some time before the wedding looking around the museum," explained Janet. "One lady saw a small boy on the third floor, which is where punishments were doled out. He actually followed her as an invisible presence as she continued her work. He kept pulling on her hair and tugging at her clothes until she was compelled to leave the event early."

Across the street from the museum is a small park overlooking the Kansas and Missouri rivers with a majestic view of the Kansas City, Missouri, skyline. It is a perfect stop for ghost tour guides to tell the story of Strawberry Hill, the haunts, and the history.

St. Mary Catholic Church

Churches invariably have haunts.

"People have an attachment to churches," noted paranormal investigator Nick Spantgos. "Many of the most important moments of our lives take place in church; baptisms, weddings, and funerals. It makes sense that a few spirits would linger in a church."

Members of St. Mary Catholic Church, located at the corner of Fifth Street and Ann Avenue, first began construction in 1890. The parish struggled to maintain membership and the church was shut down in 1980. The building still retains the original stained-glass windows, towering ceilings, and confessionals.

The current owner of the property allowed PRI to investigate for paranormal activity.

"We were excited to set up equipment and start the investigation," said Nick. "This was the first church that we had investigated so there was a high level of anticipation."

The group was not disappointed. Several EVPs were captured during the investigation.

"We heard several different voices," said Nick. "The most amazing was a cry that sounded like 'help me' in the confessional. The other voice was captured after investigator Cathy Ramirez asked, 'Was your mom pretty?' The answer recorded was 'not pretty.'"

Paranormal evidence was also displayed on the thermal imaging camera.

"Cold spots, about ten or fifteen degrees cooler than the surrounding environment, were documented on the altar," explained Nick. "Yet when we tested it later the cold spots were not found."

According to Nick, the most exciting part of the investigation involved the scaffolding. The group was taking down their equipment after the investigation "and suddenly the scaffolding slid along the wall, then hit a support column. A few of us really jumped after it happened."

Investigators are not the only ones who have experienced hauntings. Construction workers have noticed that when they arrive to work in the morning chairs have been moved into a circle in the former Sunday school rooms.

St. Mary Church is one of the top five most haunted locations in Kansas, and is a distinctive part of the downtown Kansas City architecture.

Six-Mile House

As a child attending elementary school near 55th Street and Leavenworth Road, Janet Reed recalls learning about tree rings from the hanging tree.

"The hanging tree stood near here until the late 1960s," explains Janet. "After the tree was cut down, slices [of it] were kept in the local grade school classrooms so [students] could learn how to count tree rings."

The tree was a popular and convenient place to hang horse thieves, outlaws, and other nefarious individuals, but innocent victims were also hanged from the branches.

"A traveler and his son were hanged here after bushwhackers robbed them," said Janet. "Both of their ghosts might be haunting the vicinity."

Vicious gangs used the Six Mile House as a meeting place. Owner Theodore Bartles was able to avoid arrest by local citizens simply by asking for assistance from nearby

Fort Leavenworth. Crime continued as a posse from West-port shot a Mr. Smith and captured several of his companions for stealing horses.

Bartles himself often bragged about his prowess with a gun and claimed to have defeated Wild Bill Hickok in a shooting contest. At the time Hickok was living on a farm in Shawnee.

Many years ago neighbors near the tavern believed the ghost of the robbery victims and possibly even some of the ruffians hanged from the old tree haunted the area.

Do they still haunt the vicinity today?

"I grew up in the area and have heard some of the stories," explained Janet. "Plenty of folks around here do think that it is a haunted area."

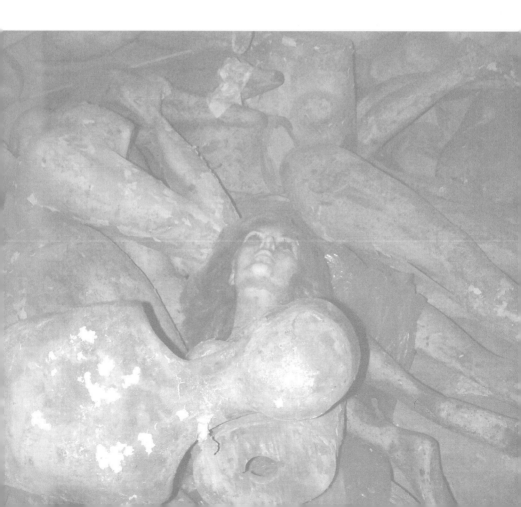

Chapter Four:

Lawrence

Lawrence is unique as a ghost tour city. This town has a psychic energy that many believe lingers from the devastating attack on the city by William Quantrill. Tom Goodrich, author of the definitive book about that famous raid, describes a moment where he stood at the corner of 7th Street and Massachusetts Avenue. By some psychic experience of his own, he became a witness to the fire-throwing men on thundering horses, mortal gunshots, and billowing smoke of the burning town. He said he truly felt that he was there…back in time 150 years ago.

An acquaintance told what at first seemed to be only a memory. Instead, her story turned out to be more evidence of the powerful physic energy of Quantrill's historic raid. Irene told us that as a little girl she lived near the Blue Mound district in Lawrence. Night after night her childhood dreams were the same fiery scenes described by Tom Goodrich… slashing raiders on horseback amidst the flames of burning buildings. These dreams occurred before she had ever learned of the historic event, and they continued for years until her family moved away.

Lawrence was established by anti-slavery and abolitionist settlers who had traveled from Massachusetts to the open prairie in the valley of the Kaw River. They established Lawrence, which grew to a population of 3,000 and became a prize plum to aggressive Missourians who were pro-slavery. Led by William Quantrill, raiders attacked Lawrence at dawn on August 21, 1863. Over 150 men were killed, including mere boys recruited for the Union army.

In 1886, a Lawrence lynch mob hanged Pete Vinegar, a black man. This stands among several post-Civil War tragedies that most believe exposed a local vein of racial prejudice. During the early 1920s, Lawrence held one of the largest Ku Klux Klan rallies in Kansas.

Today, Lawrence is among the historic Free State towns of the Kansas River Valley working with the National Park Service about its heritage based in the struggle for freedom. Its downtown "main street" and University of Kansas campus have been sensitively preserved for over 150 years.

Stubbs Mansion

A mansion that later became a college fraternity site sits majestically on Windmill Hill overlooking Lawrence. Built in 1907 by millionaire Governor William Roscoe Stubbs, the house boasted twenty-two rooms and numerous fireplaces. Descended from Quakers, Stubbs was well-known for his abhorrence of alcohol; during his governorship he cracked down on bootleggers in Southeast Kansas. The governor was considered to be a high-minded Republican untouched by scandal. Yet the legend of the mansion hints of sexual impropriety and possibly murder.

Virginia was a spirited and beautiful young lady. She caught the Governor's eye, and his Quaker heart was soon in the throes of an infatuation. He adopted her as a daughter and brought her into his home. His affection for his wife had dimmed over the years, and Virginia brought passion back to his life.

Governor Stubbs spent much of his time at the capitol in Topeka, twenty miles away. After one of his trips, he returned home the afternoon of April 21, 1911. As he climbed the stairs and reached the ballroom, he was aghast to find Virginia hanging by a rope in a closet. Was it a suicide? Stubbs sought his wife and found her sitting in her rocker, seemingly dazed and oblivious to her surroundings.

Scandal roared through the household. Mrs. Stubbs accused her husband of adultery; the governor accused his wife of murder. Heartbroken and anguished, Stubbs had Virginia's body cremated and buried behind the front hall fireplace. "The world of strife shut out, the world of love shut in" is the plaque he placed to commemorate her passing. Mrs. Stubbs was committed to an insane asylum.

By most accounts, though, Virginia has not passed — she remains an active haunt in the place where she died. The ghost stories began soon after her death.

In 1922, the Sigma Nu fraternity purchased the house and contents, and the ghost stories began to filter down through the years. The most common story is that of a ghostly woman with long hair, wearing a white dress, that can be seen looking out the window and walking the hallways.

"The world of strife shut out, the world of love shut in" marks the place where Virginia's ashes remain.

Other phenomena include flickering lights, slamming doors, and terrifying dreams.

A student relayed his own frightening story, "Late at night a light came on in my closet. Problem is, I don't have a light in my closet!" He felt transfixed as the door opened and a female figure moved towards the bed and hovered over him.

"I couldn't move," he said. "I watched her as she looked at me, and then slowly she faded away towards the door. It is not an experience that I want to repeat."

John LeRoy, a senior at the University of Kansas, had his own experiences while a resident at the house, explaining, "Somehow I was locked in my room, even though the door does not really lock...I had to bang on the door until a fellow member opened my door. It really freaked me out."

There was also an occasion when he heard footsteps outside of his door: "I heard footsteps coming down the hall, but did not see the motion detector lights come on," John said. "I went over and opened the door…it was then that the lights came on."

Skeptics point out that if Virginia really existed, death certificates and other documents would prove her death. But as some historians have noted, money and power can smooth life's inconvenient moments.

Eldridge Hotel

A hotel has stood at Seventh Street and Massachusetts Avenue since 1855; the area is considered to be the most historic corner in Lawrence. The original Free State Hotel was a wood frame structure that was burned in 1856 by Sheriff Sam Jones, a law enforcement officer who had a role in constructing the pro-slavery territorial capitol at Lecompton.

Rebuilt by Colonel Shalor Eldridge, the hotel was an imposing brick structure and was considered to be the largest and most luxurious hotel west of the Mississippi. Even western adventurer Horace Greeley called it "magnificent."

An important gathering place for social and political events associated with territorial development, Eldridge Hotel was the ultimate target for what some historians have called the first act of domestic terrorism in the United States.

The dawn of August 21, 1863, was incredibly hot. On that morning, led by William Quantrill, over four hundred Missourians approached Lawrence. With awe, they looked down at the attractive little town, populated by about 3,000 citizens. The community was by far the largest they had considered attacking during their border skirmishes. Many of them felt fear: were there soldiers and armed citizens waiting for them? The Eldridge stood like a fort of brick at the edge of the downtown. The raiders wondered if men were hiding inside, ready to bring an end to their lives, but all was quiet as the Missourians pulled their weapons from their holsters and rode into town, bringing death to over 140 men and boys while burning most of the buildings in Lawrence.

The Eldridge was rebuilt in 1865 and then again, after another fire, in 1925; staff and guests have reported haunts regularly for many years.

One of the most notable and well-documented entities is that of the "Elevator Ghost." A photo is proudly displayed in the lobby of the shadowy figure that lingers on the elevator, which often seems to act on its own accord. Guests may want to go to the basement, yet the elevator takes them to the fifth floor.

This photo of the Eldridge Hotel's elevator ghost is proudly displayed on the counter in the lobby.

"Some folks believe there is a spirit gateway on the fifth floor," explained a hotel staff member. "Room 506 has the original building cornerstone built into the wall, and the fifth floor was the top floor until Quantrill burned down the hotel."

Activity in room 506 includes misty handprints on the mirrors, lights flickering on and off, and unexplained voices. Guests often feel as though they are being watched, and there have even been reports of apparitions in the hallways. During an investigation of room 506, recording devices were mysteriously turned off while the investigators went to dinner.

Staff have also seen "card-playing" ghosts of ladies at a table in that room, apparently enjoying an afternoon game.

Through the years, deaths have occurred at the hotel, but one in particular stands out.

In 1896, during a football game between Nebraska Doane College and the University of Kansas, Bert Serf was injured with a concussion. His inert body was carried to the Eldridge as several physicians unsuccessfully tried to rouse him. Bert died of his injuries shortly before midnight. The *Lawrence Evening-Journal* reported, "Moans could be heard coming from the boy who seemed to be suffering intense pain from the injuries." Perhaps his youthful ghost is one of many that roam the hallways.

Colonel Shalor Eldridge was very proud of his hotel and several staff members believe he still enjoys a cigar in his favorite chair. That old-fashioned chair had been in a basement closet, but was recently moved to the office because it's such a curiosity. A large portrait of the Shalor Eldridge family stands above the fireplace in the lobby. Candles flanking the portrait would mysteriously begin to flame...lit not by staff, but by an unseen force.

In fact, much of the ghostly activity has been attributed to Shalor, as he continues to oversee the domain that has stood, in one form or another, majestically at the historic corner in downtown Lawrence for 150 years.

Haskell School

Haskell School was created in 1882 as a center to train and educate the youth of "noble red men." An Act of Congress in 1882 set aside schools in Kansas, Nebraska, and Oklahoma on the modern premise of putting the Government into the unique, but possibly better, business of "educating the Indians instead of killing them." Lawrence was chosen for the Kansas school location in order to acquire an education that would fit Native Americans into the community.

The first class of children began at the school in 1884. Students were stripped of their language, dress, and culture as the first step towards integration. Children were expected to perform farm work, kitchen and food preparation, road grading,

Haskell Cemetery is the resting place of the numerous children who have died in the history of the college. There have been a number of strange stories about this area.

and building construction. Food was scarce and the students often complained of short rations. During 1885-86, over five hundred incidents of illness were reported. While a few were sent home from the school, many died from disease; they were buried at the Haskell Cemetery — the youngest victim interred was Harry White Wolf, buried in 1884 at the age of six months.

Joggers on the nearby trail have heard the sound of a baby crying...yet a baby has never been found.

"I was walking back from my job to the campus when I passed by the cemetery," a student recalled. "I could hear a baby crying and asked some girls nearby to help me find the baby. They were scared and ran to the campus because they knew the baby was a ghost."

Another Haskell student also had a startling experience at the cemetery.

"For me the cemetery is a quiet place, so I come down here just to lay in the grass and think," he explained. "One afternoon I was near the big tree and could hear voices. I asked the voice to ring a little bell hanging from the tree so I would know he was there. It surprised me when the bell dinged."

The tree is a large cedar that stands in the northwest corner of the cemetery. Totems surround the trunk and hang from the branches. Native Americans still perform rituals at the cemetery, encouraging little ones that still linger to move on.

Tour guide Beth Rupert explained the rituals are meant to move the spirits upward towards Heaven. "The totems are placed around the tree to encourage the spirits," she said.

Beth further stated that the cemetery seems to be a sad place "since children are buried here" and that during a tour several visitors saw a shadow figure in the southeast corner of the cemetery.

Other paranormal activity includes visions of children playing in a nearby grassy area and misty figures seen around the trees.

The cemetery, though, is not the only location on campus with documented ghost activity...

Hiawatha Hall

Constructed in 1898, Hiawatha is the oldest building on campus. The ghostly activity there revolves around the basement.

"For many years there was a swimming pool in the basement," Beth explained, "but after a young girl drowned it was shut down."

Residents still hear the sound of splashing coming from the basement, and workmen will find their tools moved around.

Haskell Auditorium

The auditorium is noted for the ghost of a young man dressed in 1940s period clothing.

Pocahontas Hall

This dormitory seems to be a haven for several entities. Students and staff have seen a ghostly woman, described as wearing an old-fashioned long skirt and blouse, standing in the hallway. Noises and whispering voices are common throughout the hall. The basement of Pocahontas was the location of the infirmary.

Does Pocahontas dorm hold a few spirits from the school's past?

"According to students living in the hall, the basement is pretty noisy with the sounds of crying children," said Beth. "At one time it was also the morgue...students no longer have access to the basement."

Tommaney Hall

Books fall to the floor on their own volition at the library in Tommaney Hall. Library workers have seen a ghostly woman watching them near the shelves and heard their names being called, yet no one else is with them in the area. Staff have named the library ghost "Libby."

Students and staff at Haskell seem to accept the spirits, understanding in the Native American tradition that the world is more than that which is seen.

Miss Minnie's Brothel

On the bluffs above the river, quiet houses along Rhode Island Street are noisy with ghost activity.

Over one hundred years ago the Union Pacific depot was located near the Kaw; it was an easy walk up the hill to find entertainment, as at least one of the homes on the block was a brothel. The current owner has been roused from a sound sleep to the shimmying of a buxom lady.

"We call her Miss Minnie because a woman named Minnie and her sister owned this house around 1890. It may have been a brothel," explained the homeowner. "I have seen her dancing at the foot of the bed."

The ghost woman had auburn hair and wore Victorian style lingerie. She will dance provocatively at the foot of the bed... and then slowly fade away.

"The neighbor next door told me that he had filed a report with the police," continued the homeowner. "He believed that someone with red hair, in skimpy shorts and a tank top, had broken into his house. There was no evidence that anyone had broken in. I think it was the brothel ghost."

A more placid ghost also appears to reside at the former brothel house: "My husband and I have seen the specter of an elderly lady peering out the south window," said the homeowner. "She sits in her rocker as though watching the world pass by."

Sometimes the ghostly lady carries her rocking chair up and down the stairs. Recalls the homeowner, "In one particular incident I was carrying my laundry down the stairs — and I had to move out of the way while the ghost lady carried her chair up the stairs."

Another neighbor reported seeing an Indian Chief ghost in his house; a lingering reminder of those who lived along the Kaw in earlier times.

Hanging Bridge

Two ghosts have been reported on bridges that connect the north and south sides of Kaw River.

Lizzie Madden
Lizzie Madden was a troubled black woman who may have been murdered on the Northwestern Railroad Bridge. According to an account in the *Lawrence World*, November 26, 1897, titled "The Ghost Stalks Abroad," her ghost has been seen on the bridge.

A view of Kaw River and the modern bridge... The pylon of the hanging bridge can be seen in the background.

"The old Northwestern Bridge is being avoided just now. The ghost of Lizzie Madden has been repeatedly seen there. For a time this was laughed off and those who claimed to have seen it were given to understand that such fakes would not be tolerated. However, the uncanny object has been seen on several occasions by people whose word is good. These experiences have been harrowing in extreme. Those who have seen the ghost say that there is little doubt about it being the ghost of the Madden woman. Some have said that the spirit acted at times as if it were in pain and at other times as if there was a struggle. Those who have seen it are convinced that the woman was murdered and thrown in the river. There is much excitement and as a consequence the bridge is being averted after dark."

Pete Vinegar
The ghost of Pete Vinegar was also reported on the Massachusetts Avenue Bridge after his lynching.

The hanging of Pete Vinegar was a dark moment in the freethinking history of Lawrence.

Sis Vinegar, Pete's teenage daughter, was a prostitute. One of her clients was David Bausman, a wealthy older farmer who lived in the southern part of the county. Bausman met Sis regularly under the bridge; during one of their trysts she conspired with Ike King and George Robertson to rob her client. The men robbed and killed Bausman and dumped his body in the river. After the murder, Sis returned to her home with the two men.

Several days later, after discovering the body in the river, the sheriff investigated the murder and apprehended King and Robertson. Being in the "wrong place at the wrong time," Pete Vinegar was also incarcerated.

A lynch mob began to gather at the jail, eventually breaking down the building. They rounded up the suspects and lynched the three men from the bridge. "Boys, let me down easy" were the last words of Ike King, who slowly strangled to death.

Vinegar seemed resigned to his fate and, despite being an innocent man, was hanged.

Miller Hall

James Lane, Carrie Nation, and Susan B. Anthony were just a few of the notables who met in the Historic Miller Hall, located on Massachusetts Avenue in downtown Lawrence. Construction was done in several phases from 1856 to 1860. Until 1861, the second floor was an excellent meeting place for the Territorial Legislature.

The building was spared the flames of Quantrill's raid.

"Historians believe that the store owner at the time was selling stolen merchandise for Quantrill," explained Cathy Ramirez. "Miller's Hall was one of the few that was not torched."

Miller Hall was the location of the State Temperance Convention held in September 1867. Elizabeth Cady Stanton and Susan B. Anthony both attended.

Owner Josiah Miller died in 1873 of gangrene after a wagon accident in front of his general store.

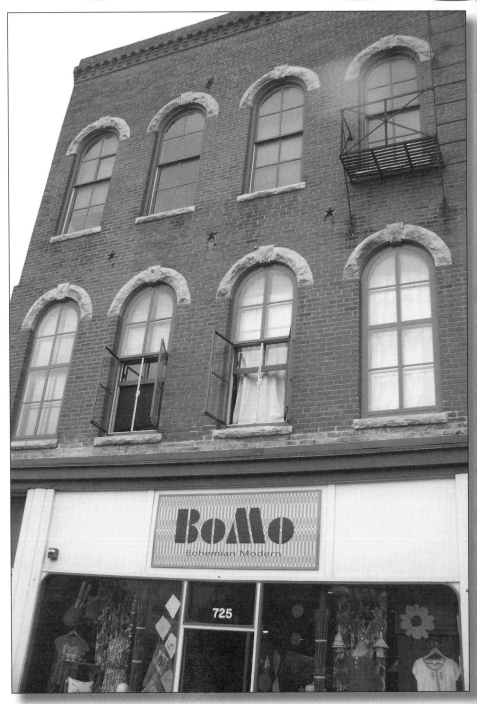

Miller Hall is one of the few buildings that was not burned and destroyed during Quantrill's Raid.

"First his foot was cut off, then up to his knee, then finally his leg," said Cathy. "Doctors were not able to stop the gangrene. That is what killed him."

Perhaps Josiah still lingers, dusting and organizing his merchandise.

Now housing the Bohemian Modern, aka BoMo, staff there have had a few unusual experiences, including one that occurred a few months after they moved in. Recalls one employee, "Objects had been moved from the shelves and dropped onto the floor."

The owner of the jewelry store next door has not had any paranormal experiences. "I wish I did have a ghost, simply because I enjoy the history of this old building," he said.

Albach House

German immigrants Philip Albach and his wife, and their children, lived in a comfortable house on Tennessee Street. The house was built around 1857; a barn on the property provided shelter for many weary travelers on the Oregon Trail that passed nearby. George, Philip's bachelor brother, lived with the family. William Quantrill was a boarder at the house for several years under an assumed name as he, unknown to the Albach household, planned his raid on the city.

That fateful morning in 1863, George had been ill and was upstairs sleeping. Raiders forced the family out of the house, shot George in the yard, and burned down the house. Accounts from the time provide a dramatic tale:

"Mr. Albach, a German, was sick in his bed. They ordered the house cleared so that they might burn it. The family carried out the sick man on the mattress, and laid him in the yard, when the rebels came out and killed him on his bed, unable to rise. These are species of cruelty to which savages have never yet attained."

Although Quantrill's orders were to preserve the house, raiders disregarded the order. Surviving family members eventually rebuilt the home on the original foundation, with further additions constructed around 1940.

Many believe George's spirit remains at his former home. Residents of the house have reported objects being moved around, with the ghost having a special fondness for keys.

"The children of the previous homeowner saw a ghostly man in a white shirt," said Cathy. "They were not afraid of him. To them, he was part of the house. Their parents believed the ghost to be George."

The children sometimes left out cookies for George; he seemed to enjoy the treats.

Chapter Five:

Leavenworth

Leavenworth is considered to be the most historic city in Kansas.

"The most compelling features of Leavenworth are the layers of experience and history," noted historian Deb Goodrich. "Not only is Leavenworth the oldest city in Kansas, but also the historic and influential role of the military post captures the pioneer movement and the essence of the West and civil struggle. A civilized community in a harsh environment."

Recently a labyrinth of former shops and offices were discovered beneath the streets. Historians and archaeologists continue to unravel the mystery of the hidden city of Leavenworth.

The history and heritage of Leavenworth are fertile grounds for ghost hunters. Historian and author John Reichley is the ghost authority of Fort Leavenworth. Evidence of the fort's paranormal activity is described in his book *The Haunted Houses of Fort Leavenworth*.

Mannequins at rest in underground Leavenworth.

Lloyd's of Leavenworth

Lloyd's of Leavenworth is an exclusive jewelry store with a ghost — *or a few ghosts*.

After ordering a custom ring, a man questioned the sales staff, "You are not alone here, are you?" The employees were uncertain as to how to respond.

When he came to pick up the ring and order a second, he told them, "There are four others here."

Staff realized the man knew about the ghosts.

The building on the corner of 5th Street and Spruce Avenue has a long history. Callahan's Drug Store was established there in 1868. In 1943, Michael Gnip purchased the store and continued it as Gnips Drug Store until his death in 1957.

"Many of the original cabinets are still in place," explained Rhonda, owner of Lloyd's. "We think that Mr. Gnip still spends time here with us."

The owner and staff have heard voices, been pushed, and seen apparitions. The activity has been occurring since the jewelry store opened twenty-five years ago.

Employees who seem to be slacking off might find themselves in trouble with Mr. Gnip's spirit.

"If the ghost thinks an employee is not working hard enough, then he will catch their attention by turning the radio on and off," explained Rhonda. "It will only stop when the employee says, 'Yes, I am working.'"

To enter Lloyd's of Leavenworth, patrons have to be buzzed in. One day while the owner was on the phone talking to a supplier, she noticed an old man standing at the door. She buzzed him in and watched while he opened the door and, using a cane, slowly walked towards the counter. When the old man reached the counter, she turned and hung up the phone. Ready to greet the gentleman, she turned back to the counter, but he was gone.

"My husband and I walked throughout the building looking for the old man. We did not find him," said Rhonda, adding, "He did not go out through the door because you have to be buzzed out. We were shocked and didn't know where he could have gone."

A similar incident took place as a woman walked past the counter and upstairs to the workshop area. The staff searched the entire building, but never found her.

"The upstairs used to be apartments," explained Rhonda. "We bricked up the outside door and now use the top floor as our workshop. There is no way she could have left the building from upstairs."

The rolling office chair seems to provide quite a bit of entertainment for the ghosts.

"When my husband is not in his office upstairs, anyone who is on the main floor will hear his chair rolling around his office," said Rhonda. "The chair moves from one wall to the next...it is almost as though the ghost is playing with it."

The paranormal activity runs the gamut from odors to display cases that move on their own. It would appear that, whether there are four ghosts or not, Lloyd's of Leavenworth certainly has enough paranormal activity to keep everyone busy...

Santa Fe Depot Diner

The Santa Fe Depot was built in 1886 and placed on the National Register of Historic Places one hundred years later. It is considered an example of the Romanesque Revival Design and made from the dark pink sandstone known as Junction City Pink. The floor plan had separate waiting rooms for men and women, common in most depots built during that time period. The depot served passengers on the LN&S rail and the Interurban passenger line. The depot was in use until 1982 and then it was abandoned.

Charles Jaster and his wife Joann purchased the property in 1983 and began restoring it. It was in a serious state of disrepair, missing most of the original architectural elements. Assisted by architects from Topeka and professional renovators, many of the original features and glass were restored to the depot.

Neil and Joyce Bitler are the current owners of the restaurant — and they are certain that a ghost haunts the former depot.

The most well-known ghost story is that of the child's hand-print that appears on the glass of the transom. Even after staff has carefully washed the glass, a handprint will re-appear.

"It doesn't matter what product is used for cleaning," said a staff member. "It always shows back up."

One explanation for that could be mineral deposits left in the glass from years ago, but some people believe the child haunting the building was one who was found murdered well over fifty years ago outside the building.

Ghostly handprints appear on the glass at the Santa Fe Depot.

"Maybe the child is leaving his mark so he won't be forgotten," suggested another staff member.

Other spirit activity includes cold spots in the dining area while patrons are eating and sounds of footsteps, voices, and eerie noises.

Two female staff members were preparing for the breakfast crowd when they heard a voice. They also both witnessed a woman in a long dress standing in the dining area before she vanished in the hallway.

Joyce, who usually opens in the morning, notices that lights will turn off behind her after she has turned them on for the day.

Kim, who spends a lot of her time in the kitchen, was working when she heard a loud, male voice say, 'Kim, come here!' Thinking it was her boss, Neil, she looked around, but realized he was in his office.

Kim also had an experience with her work cart. "I had the cart close to me, then it pulled away from me," she said. "I reached for it and it pulled away again!"

The sound of plates spinning around has also been heard in the kitchen.

A frequent haunt in the kitchen affects the sink faucet. The cold or hot water lever in the kitchen turns on at full blast and sometimes it turns back off again. The first incident occurred during the night when staff was not there. Neil came in the next morning and thought the dishwashers had left it on. Two dishwashers near the sink watched as the faucet lever turned and the water poured out.

One morning around 5:30, a waitress walking into the building from outside noticed a light on in the depot tower, which was mysterious since there is no electricity in that part of the building.

The morning staff has also found jelly packets all over the floor. Other experiences include cold brushing movements, as though being touched, and unusual noises.

While closing for the evening, an employee heard something moving behind him. He turned to look and saw a flash exit the dining room and pass through the door. The incident left his heart racing...as well as a belief in the paranormal.

A recent investigation by Paranormal Research Investigators revealed evidence of paranormal activity at the Santa Fe Depot. While down in the basement, two team members asked the entity to give them a sign that it was there. Immediately a banging noise was heard. In the same area, they asked for the entity to identify itself, and a female voice that responded to the question was recorded as an EVP.

During another investigation, team members had several personal experiences, which included hearing sticky footstep noises in the kitchen. Investigators using K-2 meters asked any spirits in the room to walk past the green light of the meter. An EVP was recorded at about the same time...a ghostly question of 'what green?'

There seems to be no disputing it: the Santa Fe Depot Diner is a great place for lunch...*and haunts*.

High Noon Saloon

The High Noon Saloon is the ghost tour headquarters for Leavenworth and might have a ghost or two, but the owners are more concerned about providing food and entertainment to patrons from both sides of the Missouri River. The history of the saloon warrants further investigation.

Leavenworth, as the oldest city in Kansas, was known for industry and commerce. Businesses thrived as the west expanded. Established in 1858, the most important and longest operated company was the Great Western Manufacturing Company.

Described in William Cutler's *History of Kansas*, the company produced such diverse products as "flour mill machinery, stationary and portable engines, saw mills, pumps, mining machinery, iron work, water wheels, and general mill furnishings. They employ 175 hands, and their buildings, of brick, cover an area of 625 square feet. The manufactures of the company are shipped all over the West, and large dealings are also had in portable flour mills, smut and separating machines, bolting cloth, rubber and leather belting, mill stones and mill furnishing goods of every description."

High Noon Saloon is the haunted tour headquarters in Leavenworth.

The Great Western Stove was one of the company's most successful products. Over one hundred styles of cooking stoves were offered across the prairie, popular with the western settlers. Today the stoves are popular with antique collectors, with the company continuing to operate in Leavenworth.

As the company outgrew or modernized buildings, they sold off properties. One of its factories is now a brewery reminiscent of the good old days in Leavenworth when there were ten breweries and sixty-three bars within a several block radius. Owners R. D. and Anna Johnson are proud of their one-of-a-kind restaurant and brewery.

"Usually it's too busy around here to pay attention to ghosts," R. D. said.

Yet, he added that the staff has had a few experiences. Sometimes the employees hear eerie noises and footsteps that can't be explained.

"Personally, I saw footsteps in the snow on the roof," explained R. D. "The roof could only be accessed by a small window, and staff had no reason to be up there. They ended at the edge. Very strange."

One of the scariest stories may or may not have been the result of a ghost.

Two female servers were working alone, finishing up for the evening. They saw a person walk through the rooms and up the stairs.

"The girls were so scared they called the police," said R. D. "The police searched the building, but did not find anyone except the Halloween cut-out of Jason Voorhees from 'Friday the Thirteenth' in the upstairs storage. I think they almost shot it…they were so startled."

The High Noon Saloon is good for a meal and as an historic site, though food may not be the only thing it serves.

Burned at the Stake

Spirits often linger where tragedy strikes; in Leavenworth, the ravine near the intersection of Lawrence Avenue and Spruce Street is one of those locations.

In November 1900, the body of Pearl Forbes was found in a wooded area several blocks from the downtown area. Fred

Alexander, a 22-year-old, was also killed at the location in a racially motivated incident witnessed by an estimated 8,000 citizens.

Two white women had been raped in a three-month time frame. Fred Alexander was accused of the second assault, that of Eva Roth, with no evidence that he had committed either crime. He professed his innocence.

The following are excerpts of the dramatic account from the *New York Times*, dated January 16, 1901, describing the scene of terror and brutality.

The Jail Broken Open

"The crowd first attempted to gain admission by peaceful means, but Sheriff Everhardy refused to deliver the Negro. Then the crowd pushed its way to a side door, and the door was forced from its hinges. Then the crowd surged into the corridor by the narrow doorway. A huge iron bar was secured and the iron door of the cell room attacked. This was finally bent so that it could be forced far enough back for the men to climb over it. Several gained entrance in this manner. In the meantime the crowd had pushed down the side gate of the stockade and in a moment there was a yelling pack in the jail yard."

"A man with sharp eyes espied a shapeless mass crouched in a corner of a dark cell, an exultant cry broke out: He is here! We've got him; bring the keys."

"The mob issued forth in a moment, dragging the Negro by the coat collar. He had been struck over the head with a hammer, but was still conscious. Men fought to get at him."

"Don't hurt him!" they cried.

"We'll burn him" was the response.

No Confession Obtained

"Confess before we harm you," they said.

"I am innocent," the Negro replied. "I am dying for what another man did. I see lots of my friends here...they know I did not do it."

"My God, men," he cried, "I am innocent!"

"He lies; Burn him!" cried the crowd.

"Take him where he committed the crime," suggested one.

At 5:15 p.m., Alexander was brought to the scene of the

murder of Pearl Forbes at the corner of Lawrence Avenue and Spruce Street. The wagon was stopped in front of the ravine and surrounded by the crowd.

"You are going to kill me whatever I say," he said, "but you men are wrong. I want to tell you right now you've got the wrong man. I did not do that, and some day you men here will run up against the man who did. I know it ain't any use to say so, for you're going to kill me, but I didn't do it."

"The Negro was quickly driven down the embankment to a pile of wood, with his hands still shackled and there he was bound to the stake.

"Coal oil was then applied for the second time, and while this was being done Alexander called to acquaintances in the crowd and said goodbye to them. He talked rationally until John Forbes lighted the match. Again, Alexander was asked to make a confession, but he replied that he had nothing to say. As the

This peaceful glade in Leavenworth was the site of horrific crimes.

flames leaped about him, Alexander turned a ghostly hue and clasping hands together, began to sway to and fro while the crowd yelled. In five minutes the Negro was hanging limp and lifeless by the chains that bound him. As soon as the crowd saw that he was extinct it began to slowly disperse. Hundreds, however, stayed to the last."

Crowd Seizes Souvenirs

"Men kept piling on wood until about 7 o'clock when the flames were allowed to go down. From 6 to 8 o'clock there was a continuous stream of people going to the scene of the burning. These were persons who had been unable to get away from their work in the afternoon and who were determined not to miss seeing the awful spectacle. When the fire had died down sufficiently to allow the crowd to approach the remains of Alexander there was a wild scramble to obtain relics. Bits of charred flesh, pieces of chain, scraps of wood, everything that could possibly serve as a souvenir was seized."

~~~~~

His father, Reverend Alexander, buried the remains of Fred Alexander at the Muncie Cemetery. No charges were brought against the mob even though an award of $500 was offered by a leading African-American group for the apprehension and conviction of anyone implicated in the murder.

The wooded ravine is quiet now, but perhaps the moans of the victims, and the roar of the crowd, still linger in this historic place.

Chapter Six:
Manhattan

A local historian described Manhattan as a "Middle town full of middle people in Middle America." The ghosts would probably disagree!

Early in 1854, as Free State settlers flocked into the state, a group of adventurers traveled up the Kansas River by steamboat. As they approached the headwaters of the Kaw, the steamboat became stranded on a sand bar. Deciding that this was a fine place to build a new town, the settlers walked up the hill and established Manhattan.

Admittedly the town does not have the drama and frontier stories that are evident in other cities on the Kaw. The historian pointed out that the proximity of Fort Riley protected the community from the violence of "Bleeding Kansas," and the vice to be found in Junction City provided necessary entertainment. Home to Kansas State University, Manhattan features limestone constructed architecture and a character all of its own.

Eureka Resort

The background of the Flint Hills Youth Job Corps facility is a fascinating mix of big ideas and good intentions initiated by the Dewey Family.

The patriarch of the family, banker C. P. Dewey, was well known in the Midwest for his land schemes, gaining most of his wealth by buying property in Chicago after the Great Fire.

In 1885, the Deweys moved to Riley County, established a bank, and acquired land through foreclosures. They owned 11,000 acres in Riley and Geary counties, which was dubbed the Dewey Ranch.

An oxbow lake that had once been a bend in the Kansas River caught Dewey's attention. The lake was nearly forty feet deep and three hundred feet wide — a perfect location for the Eureka Lake Resort.

Because Dewey enjoyed the best, the resort was extremely luxurious, comparable to the hotels in Kansas City and Chicago. Professional chefs, modern kitchens, an elegant ballroom, and fine accommodations were enjoyed by the top 150 members of Manhattan's elite.

During the flood of 1903, muddy water ripped through the resort, filling the lake with sediment.

The resort was no longer a destination; the lake was gone, and the trees and lawns were missing or damaged. Although restored, the resort never returned to its original grandeur.

The buildings were sold to the Odd Fellows Fraternity in 1906 as a retirement home for elderly members. An orphanage was added a few years later.

Fire swept through and engulfed the entire structure in 1916, claiming the life of James Burns. Another building was constructed, which the Flint Hills Job Corps uses today.

With such a colorful history, these structures are certain to be haunted... The third floor of the main building has frequent unexplained occurrences.

"We will turn off the lights and lock the doors for the evening," explained a security guard, "and by the time we have returned to our security post the lights are back on. We may do this several times before everything is secure."

Common haunts such as footsteps, voices, doors opening and closing, and banging noises can be heard throughout the buildings. Staff has also heard the ghostly sounds of children playing.

The morgue was located in the basement of the south building. Former tenants would be wheeled down there after dying and those without family were buried in the cemetery near the property.

"The ghost of a little girl can be seen looking out the window of the large brick building," said a guard. "Sometimes a child's handprint can be seen in the old gated elevator...it will appear and then disappear."

The original resort may be gone, but echoes of its existence still vibrate through its haunts.

Wolf House

The Wolf House is controversial as far as ghost stories are concerned. Currently a museum, John Frank constructed the building as a boarding house in 1868. He sold the property to a Dr. Perry and his family in 1875; they lived there for sixty-three years. Later purchased by the Wolf family, the home was turned over to the Riley County Museum in 1982.

Rumors of prostitution were an unsavory cloud over the boarding house in the early days. A death also took place within its limestone walls. A physical education teacher at the local school was injured while riding her bicycle. She was taken to her room at the boarding house in great pain, later dying of her injuries.

Museum employees are adamant that the house is not haunted. Other visitors are not so certain.

A former volunteer told us that a ghostly woman has been seen looking through the window in the upstairs bedroom. The common haunts are also evident: footsteps, objects moving around, and the sound of piano music emanating through the rooms.

While doing research, ghost tour staff found a letter in the historical society files, written many years ago by a woman named Allison. The letter provides a detailed account of a young woman who is haunting the building. According to the letter, a young girl named Elizabeth Pike was one of the first guests to arrive at the boarding house; she was found unconscious on the stagecoach. A doctor was summoned and Elizabeth had enough strength to tell her story.

Evidently, Elizabeth had fallen in love with a man named Isaac T. Collins, who went on a quest to California in search of gold and promised to marry Miss Pike on his return. During his absence, Elizabeth discovered she was pregnant; her father disowned her and kicked her out of her childhood home. She purchased her stage ticket with funds garnered by selling her mother's amethyst jewelry. No other luggage was brought except for a small locket and an oil painting of Isaac.

At first, the doctor believed her unconscious spell was due to her pregnancy. They discovered later she had tuberculosis. Eventually, Elizabeth received notice of Isaac's death.

Elizabeth bore a son, Isaac Jr., but was too heartbroken to have any interest towards the infant. She died six months after his birth.

The letter mentions a Mrs. Berry seeing a ghostly young girl, wearing a frock with half sleeves and ruffles, seated in the rocking chair.

According to tour guide Amber Munoz, the story of Elizabeth and Isaac is uncertain since it was written by a schoolgirl. However, she noted, "Whether this ghost story is true or not, it certainly is a good one."

Purple Masque Theatre

Memorial Stadium was home to the Kansas State Wildcat football team between 1922 and 1967. It later housed the Purple Masque Theatre and several other departments. Nick the ghost is rumored to spend time at the theatre.

As the story goes, back in the 1950s, a football player was injured on the field and taken into the theater, which was previously the athletics department. Shortly thereafter, the boy died of his injuries. The reality is quite a different story, since the story of Nick has moved into the realm of urban myth.

How Nick got his name is also a mystery. No students named Nick have ever died at the stadium due to football injuries, although there was one death of a student during practice. A twist to this tale is that the parents of the mortally injured player supposedly died in a terrible car crash on the way to the game to watch their son play. Some people believe the parents and the player died at the same time. There is no documentation confirming any of the incidents, but there is paranormal activity at the former stadium.

The haunts have included moving chairs and props, stomping up and down hallways, objects spinning, and levitating.

"Several people watched a stack of wood boxes falling to the floor and re-stacking themselves," said one theatre student. "Most of the time we just hear noises backstage, so the boxes were a real surprise."

One student claimed to have seen a fire extinguisher spinning in the air with foam spraying out as it spun.

A staff member believes her purse was moved around her office during the day by an unseen entity. "Every time I would need it, it would be gone, and I would have to search for it. Usually it was in an unlikely place, like a shelf or drawer," she stated.

Students and staff have seen a ghostly entity moving throughout the stadium. Three students walking up the steps saw a silhouette moving in front of them and then passing through the door. According to witnesses, one of the students noticed the door was still moving, so he peeked inside. A white misty form was still visible; the students became frightened and ran back down the stairs. The apparition has been seen moving down the hallway on previous occasions.

Banging pipes is typical in most old buildings, but at the theatre the noise is intentional. One group of students heard pipes clanging and getting louder during play practice.

One student explained that they were discussing what to do to make the noise stop, wondering if it was the ghost, when another student in the group grew so frustrated that he yelled at the ghost to be quiet. "Amazingly the pipes stopped banging after that," the student said.

Amateur investigators recorded an EVP of a male voice several years ago.

While séances are a considered a foolhardy way to communicate with spirits, a group of theatre students planned one that got out of hand. It was at Halloween, and everyone wanted to be a part of the séance.

"It was a fiasco..." said one student. "Too many people showed up and probably scared off any ghosts that might have wanted to talk to us."

The tradition of Nick the ghost will most likely continue to haunt the stadium and theater. In 2008, a tornado swept through the campus, damaging many of the buildings. It is uncertain whether Nick was injured during the storm.

Delta Sigma Phi Fraternity House

As a tour guide, it is always exciting when guests can enjoy a hands-on ghost experience. During a Manhattan tour, a group encountered more than expected while visiting the fraternity house at 1100 Fremont Street.

Originally St. Mary's Parkview Hospital, the building that houses the Delta Sigma Phi has been standing for over one hundred years — and stories of hauntings have been a part of fraternal life for nearly fifty years.

Years ago patients from the hospital were being transferred to the new Manhattan location.

Tragedy struck when patient George Segall was left behind. Segall, being weak from illness, fell between the bed and the wall, where he became wedged. Alone and helpless, he slowly died over a period of three days before he was found. Even during a final check of the building, employees saw an empty room and assumed everyone had been moved. Little did they know that George still remained, hidden from view. George still haunts his old hospital room.

Current pledges are familiar with George, as many of them have experienced his presence.

While alone on the third floor, one student walked into his room. He noticed that someone was lying under his bed sheets. Naturally, he figured a fellow was goofing with him. He responded by telling them to get out of his bed. As he reached down and grabbed the sheet, it fell flat on the bed. An unnerving experience, since no one was there.

Other paranormal incidents have taken place on a regular basis, as residents have experienced lights flickering and the sound of footsteps and what they describe as "strange and eerie noises."

During a ghost tour in 2008, a small group of guests went inside the house to view George's former hospital room and to hear stories about the haunts.

A student led the group upstairs to the far corner room, which is now used as storage for the snacks.

"One of the student's dad works at a snack company," he explained. "He sends us cookies, crackers, and chips."

The door is locked at all times in order to prevent any munchies attack. As the young man told stories about George, the doorknob rattled. Everyone became silent.

The student continued, explaining that no one should be in the room. Moments later the knob rattled again. Frowning, he announced, "I am going down to get the key...no one should be in the room."

While he was gone, Kristen, a tour guide, put her hands on her hips and said, "You can't trick us...we know about ghosts!" The knob promptly rattled again, much to the delight or concern of the group, depending on their perspective.

The student returned with a key. He and several members of the tour group went inside to investigate, but they did not find anyone in the room. The incident was attributed to the ghostly George.

One notable incident took place in 1973. After an ice storm knocked out the power lines, the fraternity was without electricity for several days. Oddly enough, though, the television would still come on at 4 p.m. every afternoon, tuned in to old "Star Trek" re-runs. No explanation could be found.

A second ghost inhabited the fraternity until the late 1960s. Students saw a ghostly nurse carrying a medicine tray in one hand and a burning candle in the other while floating down the hallway. She seemed to have disappeared; perhaps she realized that they no longer required her care.

After the group departed the fraternity house, Kristen, the tour guide, quipped: "We may as well go home because nothing will top THAT experience!"

Chapter Seven:
Shawnee

When Shawnee was suggested as a ghost tour city, the staff had some doubts. The city is ranked in the top fifty most desirable places to live in the United States. Progressive, clean, and growing... were there enough historic or notable locations with ghosts? After researching and getting some personal anecdotes, the ghost tour team was thrilled to discover a wealth of history and haunts. The ghosts of Shawnee reflect the early frontier and Native American history of the area, as well as the vibrant optimism of suburban Kansas City.

PJ's Bar

The headquarters for the Shawnee ghost tour, PJ's Bar is a popular neighborhood joint, offering folks some tasty sandwiches, poker night, and a ghost!

"We named the ghost Seymour, after Seymour Buttz," a server joked. "He is a special ghost because he seems to detect when a brawl is about to start!"

"It was the craziest thing! Something would happen behind the bar, like glasses falling, beer taps being pulled wide open, stuff moving around, and we knew to start watching the crowd," said the server. "Within thirty minutes something always happened."

Several of the employees think that Seymour is there for a purpose.

The server explained that he believed there are at least two spirits at PJ's. "I believe Seymour had something to do with keeping another spirit that I believe was not good in check," he said.

Another employee, Joyce, had an unnerving experience that she said "rattled her cage."

Last fall, while working alone in the morning, she was filling up the Yeager machine when she heard "Hope to see you Joycie" whispered into her ear.

"It was an obvious woman's voice," said Joyce. "I did not recognize the voice...I could feel a breath and hear the voice. I was here alone and did not expect to hear voices."

A former employee also shared her experiences.

"My very first (ghost) experience was after closing," said Sheila. "There were two people with me. We heard a loud voice coming from the men's room, and then the door slammed shut. No one was there when the guys went back to see what the problem was."

She had also seen the walk-in cooler door opening and closing by itself as well as shadow figures.

PJ's has been in Shawnee for a long time, so perhaps one of the loyal patrons remains...*in spirit.*

As the ghost tour headquarters in Shawnee, visitors will find there are spirits of both kinds in PJ's bar. This view is of the hallway leading to the restroom.

Downtown Shawnee

Hartman's Hardware

Located at Niemann Street and Johnson Drive, Hartman's Hardware has been a long established business in Shawnee. Three generations have operated the store for over fifty years; there is also a tradition of a ghost.

Mike Unterreiner believes that Grandpa Clarence Hartman still runs the store as a ghostly presence.

"The business was purchased in 1946," explained Mike. "The old folks used to live upstairs and run the store downstairs. Upstairs is where most of the unexplained activity happens."

The second floor is now used for storage — a plethora of nails, chemicals, and yard rakes in the midst of high ceilings, wood trim, and oak floors. You can still see the coat racks where grandpa hung his coat. The original building was constructed in 1927 as part of the Masonic dance hall.

"It is not unusual to come upstairs and find items on the floor," said Mike, "as though they were removed from the shelves or moved from one spot to another."

Mike and the staff at Hartman's aren't too worried about having a ghost in the store. If it is grandpa, he is probably keeping an eye on things.

Heaven on Earth

Heaven on Earth may be inhabited by several types of other worldly beings.

"Angels watch over me and my customers, helping them along the way," said owner Mindy Ruff. "My store is a peaceful place because of this."

Mindy describes herself as a spiritual person. She has long believed in a higher power that guides, protects, and helps her in life. Her shop and day salon are filled with images of angels, fairies, and other benevolent beings.

She also keeps a jar of angel cards. "Visitors can stop by for a reading at any time," she said.

Other entities may linger here as well.

Evidence of a haunting began with small things such as the phone ringing with no one on the other end. Although this can easily be explained, the caller ID always displays the same number: 000-000-0000. Mindy feels that it may be her lifelong best friend who passed away a few years ago.

"We used to play practical jokes on one another," she said. "It seems my friend might still be playing pranks here and at my home."

During a charitable event at the salon, a large mirror fell from the wall, making a crashing noise. Everyone was startled, certain the mirror had smashed into a million of pieces, but on examination, the mirror was leaning against the wall...*without* any breaks or cracks.

Two weeks later a similar event occurred during the night. A wreath display on the east wall was found in the middle of the floor the next morning.

Kansas City Paranormal Investigations (KCPI) has assisted in documenting the activity, and an "interview with a ghost" session was conducted in the massage room near the rear of the building.

"We documented temperature changes," said investigator Janet Reed. "As a team member was taking readings, she was gently pushed from behind. She looked behind her, but didn't see anyone."

Other slight readings were found in all three of the shampoo chairs and a photo was taken of a large orb nestled in the center chair. Joked Janet, "I guess it could be frustrating to be a female ghost and never be able to get your hair done."

Chapter Eight:
Topeka

Working and living in Topeka was an advantage for the owners of Ghost Tours of Kansas. Not only did they have a heritage of frontier and Free State history as a backdrop for their stories, but also friends, family, and co-workers were always willing to suggest locations that might be haunted, as well as provide anecdotes about ghost experiences.

The stories collected here also represent the tales of a hardy people...those who endured the struggles of pioneer settlement in Bleeding Kansas and natural disasters such as floods and tornadoes. These stories were written with pride and enjoyment.

Constitution Hall

The oldest building in Topeka — and arguably the most historically significant in all of Kansas — is also among the most haunted. According to leading historians, Constitution Hall is one of the principal landmarks standing in the American West; its events were among the sparks that ignited the Civil War.

"This building represents the pre-Civil War struggle on the Kansas Territory," explained historian Doug Wallace. "Constitution Hall-Topeka has significance at the national level."

Built in 1855, the location on Kansas Avenue represents the important events related to the Free State Movement and the drafting of the first anti-slavery constitution that took place in Topeka between 1855 and 1860.

Two of Topeka's earliest entrepreneurs, brothers Loring and John Farnsworth, built the first structure in Topeka on a high point above Kaw River. They began construction in April 1855, but were delayed when they became embroiled in anti-slavery settlement battles on the Kansas-Missouri border. Eventually the city fathers finished the stone walls so Free State delegates could meet for the Constitutional Convention in October 1855. It stood as a fortress for Topeka's early settlers, providing meeting space, storage for supplies looted from pro-slavery communities, and was the Free State militia headquarters on the James Lane Trail to freedom.

The Kansas frontier was a dangerous place, as the threat of attack was constantly on the minds of Free State settlers. Just across Kaw River to the north were the active pro-slavery settlements of North Topeka and Indianola and they strategically raided supply trains from Leavenworth and St. Joseph. Topeka suffered violent raids from these neighboring communities, with injuries and at least one death. Topekans retaliated in a pattern that continued through 1857.

Dramatic events of a nation in turmoil began to unfold at Constitution Hall. In defiance of both the federal government and a pro-slavery legislature, over four hundred Free State partisans met July 4, 1856 to banish slavery from Kansas territory. The meeting was a threat to the legislature established in

Constitution Hall is the most historic building in Topeka — and one of the most haunted in Kansas.

the pro-slavery enclave of Lecompton. Federal troops from Fort Leavenworth, led by Colonel Edward "Bull" Sumner, dispersed the meeting under threat of cannon and bloodshed. The partisans met secretly, creating one of four free-state constitutions delivered to Washington, D.C.

Through the years the building hosted many businesses, including a cutlery shop, an undertaker service, a bookshop, and a drugstore. Cy Cohen, owner of the cutlery shop, was murdered there in 1984. His ghost and many others have presented themselves during investigations.

A primary theory explaining the extreme haunting of the location relates to the Spiritualist movement in Topeka. In the 1870s, Franklin Crane, first mayor of Topeka and the developer of Topeka Cemetery, was a member of the society of spiritualists that met in Constitution Hall. Séances were a regular part of meetings; these efforts to communicate with the dead may have opened a gateway for spirits into the building—without offering a doorway out.

Paranormal investigators have spent many hours investigating and documenting the spirits of the past at Constitution Hall. Over the course of nearly twenty investigations paranormal activity has been documented, including darting red lights, footsteps, shadows, physical touching, and voices. Investigators have also collected dozens of EVP recordings...evidence that visitors are not alone in the building.

"During our first investigation, we heard a disembodied male voice saying something to us," said Nick Spantgos. "The male voice was clearly captured on the digital audio recorder, but what made this intriguing was that a thermal image captured two handprints on the wooden pillars from where the disembodied voice came from."

One of the most popular tools investigators use to measure Electro-Magnetic Frequency (EMF) is the K-2 meter. Unlike a normal EMF detector, which shows how high the frequency is through numerical readout, a K-2 meter shows differences through lights. In a normal base reading the meter shows a single green light; as frequency increases the reading moves from green to orange and then to red.

Investigators have used this unique tool to communicate with willing spirits. By asking a spirit to make the lights blink, with one blink meaning 'no' and two blinks meaning 'yes', K-2 meters have allowed the investigators to talk to different spirits that dwell in Constitution Hall.

Nick believes the K-2 meter has brought an interesting perspective to investigating the paranormal.

"The fact the meter can be manipulated to provide instantaneous results or at least provide some guidance to the area to investigate or questions to ask is absolutely amazing," he said. "The key while performing a K-2 session is to correlate the session with another piece of audio or video evidence. While performing K-2 sessions at Constitution Hall, we have also documented numerous EVPs, been tapped on the shoulder, seen shadows darting across the room, and smelled the pungent odor of pipe tobacco."

Several entities are familiar to the investigators.

Investigator Devin Cooper explained that a psychic has joined the team on investigations. With his information and the K-2 meter responses, Devin said, "We were able to identify certain active spirits."

Robert, a little girl named Cissy, Christopher, and the door guard are a few the psychic mentioned.

"We start our investigations by asking if the spirits are here and would like to talk to us," explained investigator Cathy Ramirez.

Robert is the most vocal of the entities at Constitution Hall. Most of his information was relayed through the psychic and the K-2 meter.

The ghostly Robert claims that he never received credit for his work at the Hall and this lack of recognition seems to be a sore spot for him. He also conveyed that his leg became lame during a horse and buggy accident. Robert enjoys being in the limelight during investigations…some have even called him a "meter hog."

He is very opinionated about the role of women. According to Robert, again via the psychic, women should remember their place as the weaker sex. This has led to some interesting encounters with Cathy as the primary female investigator.

"If you want Cathy to be quiet and sit in the corner, then make the meter show red and keep it red for a few seconds," requested investigator Keith Ross.

Amazingly, the meter shot up to red and stayed there. In Robert's mind, Cathy acts too much like a man, so, as requested, Cathy moved to the corner and sat quietly.

When later asked to tap on something to "give us a sign," Robert responded with three taps on an old vent.

One time during an investigation a cell phone went off; its distinctive ring tone was the University of Kansas fight song. Nick recalled that the psychic laughed and said, 'Oh, you like that?' Robert seemed to enjoy the music from the cell phone.

Another spirit is that of a little girl the psychic believes is named Cissy. She was the daughter of a prostitute who locked Cissy in her room to protect the child from clients. She is extremely shy yet is drawn towards women with blond hair, perhaps because they remind her of her mother. Cissy's voice has been captured in many EVPs and she has also made her presence known during investigations. An EVP was captured on tape of her saying, 'I want my mom.'

"During a public investigation, one of the guests began to

have unusual feelings on her right side," said Cathy. "We knew Cissy liked blonde women, and this lady was blonde. Her right arm felt chilled compared to her left, as though the ghost child was leaning against her."

Other unique experiences have taken place during investigations as well.

"My daughter Megan was sitting in a chair doing EVP recordings when an entity kicked the chair with such force that it made a loud bang and the chair was shaking," said Cathy. "We looked at each other and then left very quickly. It was a freaky experience."

Awaiting efforts for a restored Constitution Hall, ghost tours have been a unique opportunity to see where the state of Kansas really began and to contact figures whose spirits have found, almost strangely it seems, a home at this hallowed historic site.

Kansas State Capitol Building

The Kansas statehouse dome rises majestically above the downtown Topeka skyline, a symbol of the freedom and optimism of a young state that had been through the fire of civil unrest and the struggles of settlement. The day of October 7, 1866 was bound to be a fine one as visitors from around the state traveled to Topeka to see the cornerstone of the soon-to-be constructed house of government. A grand parade marched down Kansas Avenue, thrilling visitors as bands, politicians, business owners, and local citizens dressed in their finest attire walked to the east corner of the future capitol building.

The cornerstone was a 3' x 6' limestone block, hollowed out to include tokens representing the people of Kansas, including small bottles of wheat, a Bible, a piece of music donated by a piccolo player, and various other items.

A Dangerous Job

Construction did not officially begin until the spring due to the harsh winter conditions. The capitol was built in three sections; construction was completed in 1890 at a total cost of $3,200,588.92.

Nine men died during its construction.

"The first man to die at the capitol was killed when a falling brick struck his head," Cathy explained. "The work was dangerous and there were very few safety measures in place."

The third man to die was a 24-year-old ironworker named John Cave.

According to a *Topeka Daily Capital* story dated July 27, 1890, there was "A Fearful Fall" at the capitol.

"John Cave, an iron worker on the state capitol, met a frightful death yesterday afternoon about 4:30 [p.m.]. While working on the dome of the state house, he lost his balance and fell a distance of 130 feet, landing on the fourth floor of the main building and causing instant death. His skull was crushed into many pieces and his body was terribly mangled.

"Cave was one of the expert iron workers for C.R. Lane, the sub-contractor who is furnishing the iron for the dome. He was working on the top most part of the dome, sitting astride the rim, which holds the great iron ribs, which have recently been raised. With a large wrench that he held in both hands he was engaged in tightening the nut of tone of the large bolts in the top of a rib on the north side. The wrench suddenly slipped, and Cave, who had been throwing his weight with the wrench, went head first over the north side of the dome. The men who were working with him saw him fall, but were unable to help him. His body first struck the cornice on the outside of the dome, cutting his shoulder badly; he fell through the open sky light in the roof of the north wing, and in the fall struck a heavy iron rod, which crushed his skull. The first obstruction was the top terra cotta floor; his body crashed this floor down to the fourth floor where it was found a few minutes later in a terribly mangled condition. His brains had escaped from the skull and fallen through to the basement floor of the building. His left arm was broken in two places and his right leg was also broken.

"His body was taken to Barkley's undertaking establishment, where it is still held."

"Rumor has it John Cave never received his last paycheck and as a result was haunting the building," said Cathy. "Years ago, a reporter questioned state payroll about John Cave's paycheck. The response was, 'No ghosts have ever come to collect'."

A few months later another fall occurred, once again off the dome.

"A Fall to Death" headlines the *Topeka Daily Capital* story of December 10, 1890. M. Deegan was the eighth casualty of the construction project.

"Shortly after 8 o'clock yesterday morning Mr. M. Deegan, an iron worker employed by Sub-contractors C. R. Lane and company to work on the iron frame for the dome, fell from the inside diaphragm in the dome to the main floor, a distance of 120 feet, receiving instant death. He fell head foremost, clutching tight his tools and striking on his head and shoulders.

It seems that Deegan stepped upon a round piece of iron called an old man, which either rolled with him or caused him to trip, launching him to instant death.

As soon as his fellow workmen could rally from the horror of the sudden event, they hastened below to render any needed assistance. The body was removed to the undertaking establishment of J. T. Barkley on Kansas Avenue between Eighth and Ninth streets.

It was found on examination that the skull crushed near the base of the brain, both arms broken at the wrists, the right arm at the elbow, and the right leg at the knee. Several cuts were found on the face and number of contusions on the body. A messenger was immediately dispatched to notify his wife and family of their sad bereavement.

The accident was a surprise to all. Mr. Deegan, being a most careful man, had repeatedly warned his fellow workmen against recklessness and has prevented the falling of several."

Two Women Ghosts

Two women are said to haunt the capitol...for extremely different reasons.

"The most dramatic tale is that of Eileen McClain," said Cathy. "Her demise was viewed by so many people, since it occurred during a regular, busy day at the capitol. It is not very often that people see that kind of death scene."

A description of the photographs from the investigation explains the story well.

"Hey, have you seen the pictures of the lady that jumped?" was the question asked during Modesto Vasquez's lunch hour.

"I was on security duty at the museum and taking a break," explained Modesto, "and my buddy had the file of photos shot during the suicide investigation of Eileen McLain. Being a former Marine in Vietnam, it was not a problem for me to look at the photos."

The images were gruesome; the incident that triggered them was horrific.

The day of July 8, 1965, started as a regular workday for six-year employee Clyde Herron. A janitor, he received a call to cleanup a water spill near the first floor elevator.

At approximately the same time Mrs. Eileen McClain, a Veteran's Administration psychiatric patient, was on the third level of the capitol rotunda. She meticulously placed her white purse down on the marble slab 150 feet above the main floor of the capitol rotunda. Next she carefully balanced her still burning cigarette on the railing, setting it close to the pillar. She then climbed the railing and jumped to her death.

"In the photos you could see her footprints on the railing, and the shoes and cigarette were right there," said Vasquez.

As gravity pulled her towards inevitable death, her arm got caught on the second floor railing, severing the limb.

"The blood stain was on the rail, the arm was off to the side," continued Vasquez.

Clyde Herron was a lucky man that day. As he moved towards the first floor elevators, he felt something graze his arm. Eileen McClain's body came to rest on his mop bucket. If Clyde had arrived to cleanup moments earlier, there would have been two dead bodies lying on the floor of the rotunda.

"She hit the bucket with her face, it was cut around," said Modesto. "She also had multiple fractures. I had seen bloodshed in Vietnam; these photos of Eileen were really something."

The janitorial and security staffs have reported the scent of cigarette smoke wafting through the air on the third floor, yet the building is a smoke-free place. Sometimes the elevator doors open and close, as well as moves from floor to floor, seemingly on its own.

"I believe that perhaps the ghostly Eileen has decided it is safer to take the elevator than her previous choice," concluded Cathy.

Another woman haunts the capitol, but her story is less dramatic than the others. Rather, it's a good example of a dedicated state employee.

Within the studious confines of the Kansas State Capitol Library, employees believe that Louise McNeal, the third librarian for the State of Kansas, is haunting her former workplace. Louise worked at the library for thirty-six years until she was forced into retirement; a table was set up for her

View of the library at the state capitol... The former librarian is believed to be haunting the room.

because she still enjoyed being a volunteer. She died within two years of retiring. It was noted in the *Kansas Library Bulletin* that "Miss Louise McNeal, State Librarian from July 1, 1926, until her retirement in 1962, died on August 6, 1965, in Topeka. Miss McNeal devoted her life to Kansas libraries and probably did more to promote their growth than any other person."

Employees, especially those working alone or working late in the evening, have experienced books moving around or falling off the shelves and chairs being pushed into the tables.

"I had just finished vacuuming half of the library and was getting ready for the other half when I heard the loudest commotion," said Lou Ann, one of the nighttime custodial staff. "It sounded like furniture being moved and books hitting the floor. I was so scared I did not even finish cleaning the library...I locked the door and left."

On another occasion, she had just stepped inside the door when the clock hanging on the wall fell down, landing near her feet.

"That was a surprise, to see the clock on the floor," said Lou Ann. "I figured that the ghost was letting me know she was there."

While people like to joke about "dead political careers" lingering at the capitol, it is not difficult to imagine that although the capitol is a beautiful, majestic old building, there is a death cloud that hangs over its existence.

Brothel History

One of the stops during the downtown Topeka ghost tour is located across from the Capitol. Although the somewhat more respectable Kansas Judicial Center stands on the grounds now, in the late 1800s the Red Light District, also called the "Peach Orchard," could be found in this area. According to police records, the women were a rowdy bunch. During raids, the girls would fight back with pistols drawn.

"One woman had a shoot-out with the cops, ran out of bullets, and jumped out of the window, trying to escape," said tour guide Megan Ramirez. "She was eventually captured in a snowdrift by police."

During the mid-1900s, the Red Light District was on South Kansas Avenue between Third and Sixth streets. The most notorious location was the old Norva Hotel.

"A gentleman on our tour told us how he had worked at Sears for twenty years," explained Megan. "Like clockwork, Mabel, the madam of the hotel, would come in once a month and buy twelve new mattresses with cash. As soon as she hit the front door, Mabel would start yelling his name so she could buy mattresses."

The Norva was torn down in 1977.

"Today's Red Light district is still close to downtown, near Topeka Avenue," said Megan. "The common factor between all of the areas is their proximity to the Capitol. After all, the women followed the money and, in Topeka, the money is at the Capitol."

Topeka High School

In 1893, Topekans were embarrassed at the condition of their high school. Topeka High School had been relocated from five different buildings over the course of twenty-three years. Those buildings included a business block, the old Washburn Academy Building, and the Hudson Building.

After 1893, Topeka High moved to its current location. By 1905 a second building, the south building, was constructed across the street in order to accommodate the growing student population. The street had to be shut down between classes in order for students to cross safely.

The buildings were dark and cramped, with classes held in hallways. The fire marshal condemned the older North Building. The library was known as the 'woodshed', as it was a portable building that could be moved around when needed.

In 1928, officials made the decision to build a new high school for the district. The architectural firm of Thomas Williamson was hired and plans were drawn. During construction a few details were added without the knowledge of the architects. In most of the classrooms there are shelves and storage units set into the walls; originally the plans called for the extra storage in a few specific rooms. In order to continue their employment, workers intentionally included shelving in every room.

The Gothic-Tudor building was opened to students in 1931. Topeka High School has become a proud landmark for Topeka, and students and faculty are proud of the school where they work and learn.

Rumors of the school being haunted have existed for a long time. The majority of the stories are from the ROTC storage and classrooms and the theater.

Hoehner Auditorium has several ghost stories attached to it. During one incident, photography students left a camera behind on the stage. Returning later, they found that three photos had been taken, two of which included orbs.

In the workshop where costumes and props are built and designed, there is a heavy door separating the workshop from the back hallway and drama classrooms. Adam, a former student, enjoyed working in the theater during the majority of his high school career. He claims to have seen the heavy door close right in front of him by itself.

"I watch TAPS," he explained. "I debunked it the best I could. A breeze could not close it."

A drama teacher found herself in the dark while in the restroom. Although alone in the area, something turned off the lights. Thinking that pranksters might be outside the door, she ran out, but no one was there.

One student claimed that her hair had been pulled as she walked on the mezzanine; some have reported something grabbing at their ankles.

Under the stage is a crawl space where theater students test their bravery. One young actress was made to crawl in and actually heard a disembodied voice calling her name. Custodians who clean the school during the night claim to hear banging on the stage when they are alone in the building.

"When I was working here alone, I would hear doors slamming in the halls," mentioned a former security guard. "I told myself they were only the radiators so I wouldn't freak out."

Other activity includes swinging padlocks on the lockers and erratic elevator movements.

"I have heard noises, banging, and sounds in the library," said a custodian. "These are noises that just don't sound like a shifting building."

Two students claimed to have seen an apparition in the loft above the library. The girls said it was a woman wearing a light colored blouse and she was peering down at them.

Ghost stories in the theater are well known at Topeka High School.

Students have also reported hearing footsteps pacing back and forth in the ROTC storage room. One experience was so startling, a student left early.

"I was here on a Sunday afternoon, folding towels in the classroom," said the male student. "I heard a loud bang and saw that the door had slammed shut. There was no breeze, and it is too heavy to shut on its own."

Activity has occurred in other classrooms. One teacher said that she watched as objects on her desk moved of their own accord during class.

The school has a rich tapestry of stories to go with the haunts, which doesn't seem to faze the students any.

"Students here love the tales of ghosts," said tour guide Devin Cooper, also a former student at Topeka. "Teachers may deny that spirits are in the school, but students have created stories from haunted mash potatoes to a ghost of a woman in the tower."

No one has any conclusive evidence of whether Topeka High is truly haunted.

However, there is a very unique photo mounted on the foyer wall. The image was taken in September 1931 before the school opened; it shows the foyer and silhouettes of two women standing in the hallway. What makes the photo unique is that the women have a ghostly or transparent appearance.

Whether a skeptic or a believer, there's no doubt the community is proud of its high school.

Seaman School District

Young people have vivid imaginations and are not immune to the thrilling idea of having a ghost in their school. Sometimes imagination and fact collide — and the result can be some fascinating stories of paranormal activity.

Leon the ghost might be haunting three of the district's schools: two of its elementary schools and Seaman High School.

Leon was a maintenance employee contracted to do basic repairs at all of the district schools. A jovial man, Leon was well liked by teachers and staff. Leon died in a tragic auto accident, killed by a drunk driver on State Highway 40.

"I believe it is Leon because the ghost acts just like Leon while he was living," explained Shirley, who worked at two district elementary schools, one of which is now closed. "Things happen in the kitchen that have no explanation, so we think that Leon is trying to get our attention."

Shirley and Elsa both worked in the kitchen at the former school, which had been built in 1950 and closed in 2009.

Elsa was the first to arrive in the morning. Her routine began with turning on the radio.

"One morning I turned the radio on to my favorite country station, then suddenly it switched to a rock station," said Elsa. "I switched it back to country and it switched again to rock. After a while I decided to just leave it on the rock station, figuring that Leon just didn't want to listen to country!"

Elsa, though, refused to go into the food storage closet by herself. "I have heard cans moving around on the shelves and whispering voices," she said.

Cathy, another kitchen employee, fetched items for Elsa out of the back room. Dee Dee, the kitchen manager, watched as cans rolled off the shelves in the storage room…yet the shelves had a lip in order to prevent rolling.

"I have had my own share of experiences," said Cathy. "One of my first was the commercial floor mixer emblem went flying off of the mixer and ended up on the floor several feet away. The mixer was not being used, and we have no reason why it happened. Sometimes, the mixing beaters rattled around in the bottom of the bowl by themselves."

Yet another incident reminded the kitchen staff that they were not alone…

While taking a break in the main cafeteria, the lunch ladies heard a loud crash coming from the kitchen area. Since the room was supposed to be unoccupied, they went in as a group. They discovered a large cup of ice water on the floor, yet no one was there.

"What made this incident interesting was the fact that the condensation ring left on the stainless steel counter was in a perfect circle," said Cathy. "It was as though the cup had been picked straight up and thrown on the floor."

While sitting at her desk taking care of daily paperwork, Dee Dee heard an unexpected click near the rows of lockers behind her. As she turned to look, a locker door was open and objects were falling to the floor. Perhaps this was another way for Leon to catch the attention of the staff.

Rochester Elementary

Shirley worked at the Rochester school for over twenty years and was Leon's friend.

"Leon is as annoying as a ghost as he was when he was alive," laughed Shirley. "He is still doing the same things, like pulling my hair or poking me in the neck."

She still feels his ghostly presence. One time, for example, Shirley had her hands full while trying to enter a classroom.

"I watched as the door knob turned and the door opened," explained Shirley. "It closed behind me. I thanked Leon for being so helpful."

Seaman High School

Leon has also been spotted at Seaman High School. Scott, a delivery driver and maintenance guy, was also acquainted with Leon.

"I saw a dark silhouette at the end of the room that looked like Leon," said Scott. "Then, when I went out to get some more tools from the truck, I could hear my name being called. My buddy was working in another part of the building, so I think it may have been the ghostly Leon trying to talk to me."

Other School Ghosts

Leon is not the only ghost haunting the schools.

At the former elementary school, teachers had seen a ghostly pioneer woman. Said Elsa, "I was standing close to the pan racks, and my attention was caught by the figure of a pioneer woman standing to the left of me."

The entity was wearing a long print dress and a bonnet. The former school happens to sit on the Oregon Trail; staff theorize that the woman may have died here during the long journey west. Historians believe that as deaths occurred along the trail there was neither time nor a location to bury the bodies. It was common practice to dig graves between the wagon rut tracks. Here the ground had been well trampled upon, ensuring a grave deep enough to prevent scavengers from digging up the corpse.

A more recent ghost haunting occurred in May 2008. Just a few days before her sixth grade graduation, a young girl was tragically killed in a car wreck not far from the site of the former school. While preparing for students to return to school in the fall, two teachers experienced paranormal activity that they attributed to the ghost of the little girl.

Each teacher was alone in their classroom when the incidents took place.

The first teacher heard the distinct sounds of a little girl giggling and laughing, yet no one else was in the room.

The second teacher, though alone in her classroom, suddenly felt as though someone had walked up behind her, wrapped their arms around her waist, and gave her a big hug. Each of these teachers had taught the child in their classroom during her school years and both remembered her to be an affectionate child.

The milk deliveryman also had an experienced at the former school.

The school was quiet on Saturday mornings when he made his delivery, entering through the side door. On three occasions over an eight-year period he saw the full image of a small girl. He described her as dressed in 1950s style clothing. She stood at the end of the hall, disappearing as he approached with his cart full of milk.

Since that particular elementary school closed in 2009 as part of a district consolidation program, it's safe to say that only the ghosts roam these quiet hallways now.

Maynard Takes the Cake

In 1912, young Robert Maynard began his life career as a baker under the watchful eye of his aunt and mother at their downtown Topeka café and bakery. Later, Robert and wife Ida Lee established a successful restaurant featuring baked ham, chicken, and Swiss steak meals, plus a dessert for just fifty cents. Locals enjoyed the good food and cozy environment at Maynard's.

In 1973, the Maynards moved their shop to Gage Center in Topeka, retiring three years later after fifty-two years in the bakery and restaurant business. In an interview for the *Topeka*

Capitol-Journal, Maynard stated, "I'd die for my business; I'd lie for it and I'd steal for it—and I am an honest man." Robert Maynard did not die for his business, but his spirit still lingers at Gage Center.

Allyson Fiander, pastry chef and co-owner of Daddy Cakes bakery in Gage Center, studied pastry and bread baking in France and trained at the San Francisco Baking Institute. According to Allyson, they "go where no cake has gone before. Daddy Cakes are real, original, and fun. This isn't fake cake."

Always ready to assist customers, she was startled when one particular gentleman seemed to linger near the front door. "He would stand briefly on the right side of the glass and then would disappear," she noted. "I didn't think too much about it until I saw his picture in the newspaper story."

The photo in the paper was of an older man with glasses and thinning hair. "It was fascinating to see the image of the man in the picture was the same as the man who lingered by my front door!" Allyson exclaimed. That man was Robert Maynard.

After doing some research, a local historian suggested the possibility that Maynard was haunting the location. After all, he did enjoy good food and had a bakery in the vicinity of the current shop.

Some other indications of a ghost were noticed by the staff: they have seen reflections in the equipment, as though someone had stood behind them; pictures fall off of the walls, and potholders and pans fall to the floor. Most common are the footsteps and the doors opening without the assistance of a customer.

Allyson named a cupcake after Robert Maynard. "He seemed to be a nice man, and I wanted to dedicate a treat that he could appreciate."

Moose Lodge

Constructed in 1954, several generations of North Topekans have enjoyed entertainment and fellowship at the Moose Lodge. Current members often reminisce about dances and dinners held in the early days of the club.

"We came here for dance parties when I was a teenager," recalled an elderly patron. "It was so much fun to dress up and dance. Now my grandchildren come with me for the pancake feeds."

It seems that a few folks hanging around may not be official card-carrying members of the Lodge.

"Yes, we have some ghosts, no doubt about it!" confirmed Richard, a long-time member of the Moose Lodge. "I have personally experienced a ghost in the kitchen, and people have wild stories about the sofa ghost. We also think that the ghost of a police officer shot on the roof is here."

The Honest Policeman

The police officer was Clarence Boots Shields, and his was one of the more intriguing crime stories in Topeka history.

Shields, a six-year officer of the Topeka Police Department, also ran a successful trucking company while off-duty. He was well-respected as an officer and known throughout the city as an honorable man.

On Monday, April 11, 1955, Officer Shields interrupted a burglary in progress on the roof of the Moose Lodge. He was shot and killed...his patrol car found abandoned several miles away from the crime scene. His body was found later in North Topeka.

This story made headlines because the two robbers claimed the officer was part of the heist and that he had been killed as the three argued about dividing the spoils. Both of the suspects worked for Shields at his trucking company, fueling the speculation that the patrolman had a role in the crime. During the trial one of the robbers finally admitted that Shields was not part of the heist; they had acted alone. The gunman was convicted of first-degree murder and spent the rest of his life in prison, while the other suspect was convicted of second-degree murder and sentenced to fifteen years in prison.

"Over the years the ghost of Clarence Shields has been seen—or heard—at the Moose," said tour guide Cathy Ramirez. "People have seen him on the roof, or heard footsteps walking on the roof."

A few years after the incident, one of the neighbors in the residential area near the Moose revealed she had seen the patrolman's ghost on the rooftop and on the north side of the building.

"The claim caused her much grief...people made fun of her about what she had seen," said Cathy. "Eventually she ended up in the mental institution after an emotional breakdown, refusing to speak about what she had seen."

It is not uncommon for staff and visitors to hear ghostly footsteps on the roof...many believe it's just Clarence, re-living those final moments as a police officer.

The Sofa Ghost

Other ghosts linger at the Moose Lodge; one in particular seems to be attached to furniture.

Years ago a sofa and chair belonging to a deceased member were donated to the lodge. The chair was placed in the ladies restroom and the couch in the front entryway.

"My mother Dorothy and I have seen the ghostly old lady," said Cheryl. "She used to sit in the chair...we could see her reflection in the mirror."

The ladies, both staff members at the Moose, described the ghost lady as being "very petite, the top of her head not reaching the top of the chair, wearing a knee length print dress, dark shoes and her hair was in a bun."

The sofa in the children's playroom at the Moose Lodge... members have seen a ghostly old woman hanging out there.

The ghostly old lady was most often seen early in the morning while Cheryl or Dorothy were cleaning the bathroom.

"I know there were times that she did not think we were doing a good job cleaning," said Cheryl.

The ghostly woman would appear while the mirror was being wiped down.

"The lights would start to flicker and then we could see her reflection in the mirror, sitting in the chair," explained Cheryl. "One time I set the trash on the chair and it went flying across the room."

The haunting took a turn for the worse while Dorothy was cleaning the restroom. As usual, the lights flickered and the ghostly old lady presented herself while Dorothy was cleaning the mirror. Suddenly the lights shut off completely, panicking Dorothy as she felt her way for the light switch. She flipped the switch, but the light did not come on. She found the doorknob, but the door would not open. Knowing that the door did not lock, Dorothy started screaming; Cheryl heard her and came to open the door. Oddly, a chair was propped on the outside of the door — how the chair became positioned against the door is a mystery, since no one else was in the building. The chair was immediately removed from the building.

"After we removed the chair, we figured the old lady would be gone," said Cheryl. "We had forgotten about the couch in the front entry...the ghostly old lady moved from the chair to the couch."

There was evidence that the ghost still lingered. Door locks stopped working in the office, and members and employees started to see a shadow figure in the front area.

About a year ago, several men were having a private meeting; two of the gentlemen came out to the foyer to stretch their legs. Standing in front of them was a woman holding a camera.

"We did not know how the woman could have gotten into the building; all of the doors were locked. We asked her what she was doing and how she had gotten into the building," said one of the gentlemen. "She explained to us that she was taking a picture of the little old lady on the couch. You can imagine our surprise when we turned to look at the couch and saw nothing, then turned around and saw that the woman with the camera had disappeared... Now we have a ghostly woman with a camera taking a picture of the ghostly woman on the couch!"

The sofa is now located in the children's play area. Several children of various ages were interviewed and they all agreed: We know [the old lady] is here and she seems very nice.

Other Ghostly Specters

Bingo is one of the entertainment attractions at the Moose. One member had a visual encounter with a spirit in the entryway during bingo night.

"I was playing bingo in the large room near the doors when I noticed a dark shadowy figure in the foyer," she explained. "I looked again and started elbowing the lady next to me to find out if she could also see the shadow." Both women claimed to have seen the figure.

The kitchen is another active location for a ghost. While working in the kitchen, Richard has had physical encounters such as cold spots, spirits actually passing through him, and the usual haunted happenings of lights flickering, radio volume up and down, appliances off and on, unusual noises, and items disappearing.

PRI and a psychic recently did an investigation, focusing on the kitchen. Laughed Nick, "One of the funnier moments happened when the psychic told the team that a ghost was cussing profusely at us."

Moose Lodge members enjoy their ghosts, figuring that they are fellow members...*there in spirit*, if not in body.

Downtown Sandwich Shop

Palmer's Undertaking Service was located at 809 South Kansas Avenue for many years.

"At any given time on North or South Kansas Avenue, you could find as many as ten or twelve undertakers within a several block radius of the downtown areas on both sides of the river," explained Cathy Ramirez. "Undertaking was big business!"

Current employees believe ghosts are haunting the former mortuary, which is now a sandwich shop. One in particular they decided to name George.

"George was randomly chosen by the staff as a good name for the ghost," said Cathy.

What makes the story interesting is that later a young woman presented an old newspaper article to the employees. The article was about her great-grandfather's business that stood at the location prior to it being a sandwich shop.

The name of the business was George Palmer's Undertaking Service.

Employees Sandy, Brenda, and Eric have had many encounters with George.

"George seemed to spend most of his time in the basement and would react differently with different staff," Cathy noted. "If Eric was in the basement, George would make footstep noises behind him; if Brenda was in the basement, George would knock things off the shelves or push things out in front of her as she was walking. George must have been very fond of Sandy. He seemed to always be by her side or pass through her as she would be coming down to the basement."

On one occasion Sandy was downstairs counting money as she closed for the evening.

"I was the only one in the shop and it was really quiet. Someone coughed behind me," said Sandy. "I knew it was George the ghost, but the incident was enough to make me put the money in the safe and wait until the next day to finish up."

George disappeared for a while after a fire damaged the basement. Sandy believed he had moved on...until recently. When staff reported hearing a man coughing in the main dining area of the sandwich shop, everyone agreed — George was back!

George is not the only ghost here at the shop.

One Saturday morning, Sandy and Brenda were preparing the shop for the lunch crowd; Sandy was behind the counter while Brenda was arranging the tables and chairs.

Both were surprised as they watched a ghostly woman dressed in Victorian attire pass through the north wall, float across the room, and exit through the south wall.

"We looked at each other and in unison asked if we saw that," said Sandy. "We both saw that she was wearing a shawl, dark skirt, and blouse."

On another occasion, staff arrived in the morning and noticed that during the night sugar had been used to create bug shapes on the tables.

"Everyone seems to agree...you never eat alone at the sandwich shop," concluded Cathy.

Marion Lane Candles

One of the ghosts at Marion Lane Candles seems to like the owner, Connie Cook.

"I rarely go upstairs to the third floor storage area," she said. "Since I am the only person with a key to the room, it was a major surprise to see 'Hi Connie' written into the dust on an old window leaning against the wall."

The ghost makes its presence known in many ways at the shop located in downtown Topeka.

One day Connie and an employee were standing by the counter talking when the card rack started spinning.

"There was no one else in the store, and we were really surprised when the display rack started spinning in circles," explained Connie. "I guess we have started to get used to some of the crazy things that happen around here."

Along with the usual footsteps and sounds associated with haunts, the ghost at Marion Lane dings the customer bell above the front door. The door has also opened and closed as though a ghostly customer is walking across the threshold.

The basement ghost often resists staff at closing.

"Sometimes after we have shut off the basement lights and start to close the door it seems that something is pushing against the door, as though to keep us from shutting it," one staff member reported. "Most of the time we ask the spirit to let us close the door so we can go home. Then the door will close, and we can finish our work."

Not all of the spirits at the store are friendly. Connie had a negative experience on the second floor that made her feel very uneasy. After a rainstorm she went upstairs to check on a possible leak in the roof. As she walked across the room, she felt a dark presence surrounding her.

"It is hard to explain, but as I walked I could feel myself slowing down to the point that I was barely moving," Connie recalled. "It felt like something bad was stopping me, or trying to take away my energy. I don't go up there anymore by myself. It was a scary experience."

Her friend Dianne Lawson, an astrologer and Feng Shui professional, confirmed what happened.

"When I was with Connie on the second floor, I felt the hackles go up on the back of my neck. I had heard of that phenomenon before, but had never experienced it. I felt afraid and knew there was some presence or energy…something not good that was surrounding me. All I wanted to do was leave immediately. It is hard to describe what I felt, but I knew that it was real and was dark and negative."

"Connie told me that where I felt that presence was the same place she had her experience," said Dianne. "Because I am an astrologer and a Feng Shui consultant who works with energies, I have heard about and experienced many strange phenomena, but nothing that was so negative and so enveloping."

During an investigation by PRI, member Devin Cooper saw a moving shadow on the third floor.

"There used to be offices up here…the names are still on the doors," said Devin. "I saw a shadow moving in the far corner of the beauty parlor. It was more of an annoyance since I could not get a good look at the shadow or what could cause it."

Near the former dentist office Devin and Nick shared a paranormal experience. "Something tipped over Nick's recorder and holder," said Devin. "It made a loud noise and caused us to jump! We believe the entity may have tipped it over."

The most exciting occurrence during the investigation took place when Nick saw a figure standing in the doorway of the beauty parlor. He had just completed a sweep of the hallway with the thermal imaging camera and noticed a figure in the doorway next to him. Thinking it was a reflection, he did not pay attention to it until later when he realized that the door was open…and there was no reflective surface.

During the investigation ribbons helped to indicate a presence was in the basement.

"We were in the basement, sitting in the dark and recording for EVPs," said investigator Cathy Ramirez. "I felt something brush my face and arm and discovered that a red ribbon was laying across my lap. There was no way it could have blown or fallen by accident...it was paranormal."

Evidence of a ghost has been around for a while. Prior to being a candle shop, the location was a shoe store. Extra inventory was stored in the basement; sometimes the owner would open in the mornings to find shoes and boxes all over the floor...as if someone went along and flipped them off the shelves.

Connie and her staff are proud of the store and are always happy to share stories of their candles—and their ghosts.

Mills Building

Constructed in 1912, the Mills building was the first steel structure in Topeka. Pelletier's Department Store, a Topeka mainstay for over fifty years, was located on the lower floors, with medical offices upstairs. The building is now the home for state offices.

During the 1966 tornado, all of the windows in the building were blown out from the storm.

According to tour guide Cathy Ramirez, "Rescue workers filtering through debris would see a hand sticking up from the rubble. When they reached down to pull it out, they discovered it was attached to a display mannequin from Pellitiers."

The mannequins might be gone, but there are a few ghosts that linger at the Mills building.

The ghost of a twelve-year-old girl has been seen by state employees on the fifth floor staircase as they are leaving for the day.

Other staff members have had a paranormal experience in the second floor break room.

"One lady was in there making coffee. She thought someone was standing behind her, but when she turned and said hello, no one was there," said tour guide Megan Ramirez. "She felt a cold presence move through her...she was disturbed by the experience."

The elevator seems to be another active location, as the doors open and close on their own and move floor to floor without purpose.

"Since spirits linger in places they enjoyed spending time, there must have been a lot of happy shoppers here at the old Pellitiers!" concluded Cathy.

Kansan Hotel

Elvis Presley was the biggest star that spent the night at the Kansan Hotel. On May 21, 1956, Elvis performed at the Municipal Auditorium to the delight of 2,500 fans. He rented the entire ninth floor of the hotel and then performed an impromptu concert party at the rooftop garden and ballroom.

"All that I remember about the Elvis show were all of the screaming girls," recalled one old-timer.

The Kansan Hotel was constructed in 1924, at a cost of nearly $1 million dollars. The hotel closed in 1968; the building was renovated into a bank and apartments. In its former glory, the hotel was one of the finest and most elegant places in Kansas.

The Kansan Hotel was extremely upscale...with some less than upscale activities.

"Women came here in the early days to have a certain procedure done," explained tour guide Cathy Ramirez. "One woman in particular is believed to be haunting the building as she looks for her baby; she had died as a result of the surgery."

Another ghost is believed to be that of a kidnapper who held a salesman hostage at gunpoint in his room. Police surrounded the hotel, tossing tear gas into the room. Realizing he had no chance of escape, the kidnapper committed suicide.

A current tenant who lives in one of the apartments has a ghost as a roommate.

"The lady who lived in the apartment before me died here," she said. "I see her ghost walk through the rooms once in a while. It does not bother me a bit."

Other haunts in the building can be attributed to the fact that Barkley's Undertaking Service operated on the property before the hotel was built.

Hotel Jayhawk

Hotel Jayhawk, constructed in 1926, was an elegant hotel and popular with celebrities, politicians, and Topeka socialites.

Conveniently located near the capitol, legislators would meet in the Senate room for cocktails and political intrigue; in fact the most nefarious scheme in Kansas political history collapsed at the Jayhawk Hotel. The scandal broke in 1933, leading to financial ruin and suicide.

W. W. Finney and his son Ronald were very friendly with some very important men of the time, including Governor Alf Landon and newspaper editor William Allen White, and were major contributors to Landon's campaign for governor in 1932.

"Both men were considered to be great guys and were very popular," explained Cathy. "What most people didn't know was the fact that they were crooks and were stealing money from the state."

The Finneys operated a securities business, but by 1933 it was discovered that Ronald had been forging municipal bonds. The scandal broke when authorities realized that State Treasurer TD Boyd had provided Ronald access to the state treasury.

"Ronald was stealing bonds from the state treasury and re-placing them with forgeries," said Cathy. "Later it was revealed that the attorney general and the state auditor for Kansas were also in on the deal."

Governor Landon declared martial law at the capitol and called for a special session of the legislature to deal with the crisis. Although an attempt was made for impeachment, both the attorney general and the auditor remained in office due to party politics.

Ronald Finney was sentenced to prison for thirty to six hundred years, but he was paroled after twelve years. His father W. W. Finney committed suicide, unable to face the humiliation of the trial and prison.

"Although it was quite a scandal, party politics held true so the Republicans remained unscathed by the incident," Cathy noted. "Landon was re-elected governor, then ran unsuccessfully for president."

Hollywood stars have stayed at Hotel Jayhawk when performing next door at the theater. The register documents Groucho Marx, Sally Rand, Robert Young, Bing Crosby, Robert Mitchum, Roy Rogers, and Dale Evans.

The rooftop garden and party room were popular and beautiful locations for proms and weddings.

Just recently a family gathered in the lobby of the Jayhawk, taking photos and enjoying the history of the building.

"We are visiting...it is our fiftieth wedding anniversary," exclaimed the matriarch of the group.

They had already experienced the paranormal during their brief visit. "We got on the elevator and pushed the button for the third floor," the lady explained, "but instead of stopping on the third floor it went on to the seventh."

The maintenance staff concur that the elevator seems to have a mind of its own.

"Yes, the seventh floor seems to get quite a few stops, whether there are people on the elevator or not," said a daytime maintenance man.

This is attributed to the ghostly young woman in the white gown, and she is only one of several ghosts haunting the former hotel.

"The story is that in the mid-1920s a young lady attending a party on the rooftop later jumped from the window of her room on the seventh floor," said Cathy. "Her body was discovered in the alley near the manhole cover."

The building staff have watched as a ghostly young woman in party clothes smiles at them before the elevator doors close, then stops on the seventh floor. The elevator then returns to the lobby...without a passenger.

This view of the lobby of the former Hotel Jayhawk shows the elevator where a ghostly woman has been observed.

Another ghostly entity enjoys spending time in the Senate room.

"Several people have seen a ghostly woman walking from the Senate room down the hallway," explained Cathy. "Staff have also mentioned that before meals, place settings were moved around and not in proper order."

The Jayhawk Hotel has been renovated as an office building and is on the national historic register, and the neon "Jayhawk Hotel" sign continues to glow on the rooftop.

Jayhawk Theatre

Topeka is known for many things, including tornadoes, civil rights, politics, and...strippers!

In December 1928, a traveling vaudeville entourage arrived at the Jayhawk Theatre for another show. Mother Rose and her two daughters, June and Louise, prepared for a successful evening on stage. Trouble was brewing behind the scenes as June, hours away from going on stage, eloped with a young man named Bobby. Mother Rose was furious; she caught up with the young couple. Pulling out her pistol, she aimed it at her new son-in-law. She pulled the trigger several times, but luckily her efforts were deterred by the safety lock.

It was up to Louise to step onstage and replace her sister; overnight the legendary Gypsy Rose Lee was born at the Jayhawk Theatre. She became the most famous burlesque performer in the United States.

When it was constructed in 1925, the theatre offered luxury that guaranteed "every seat the best seat in the house" and air-conditioned comfort to patrons. And, indeed, it was luxury to spend a Saturday afternoon watching the talkies, out of the hot Kansas summer sun.

Theatres often have haunts — and the Jayhawk Theatre is no exception.

"Love, pain, hope, and fear...all elements of the human condition are played out in the theater," noted Janet Reed, a tour guide and paranormal investigator. "Spirits might be attracted to this type of energy."

One ghost is believed to be that of a traveling salesman.

It is not unusual for young people to meet and fall in love at their workplace. In the case of the Jayhawk Theatre, an usher and an attractive young lady who handled the tickets appeared to be a couple, enjoying each other's company and planning for the future — or so the young man thought.

However, the girlfriend was also involved with a traveling salesman. The salesman, who had stayed at the Hotel Jayhawk when visiting Topeka, met the young lady during a movie. He was smitten and saw her as often as possible.

The usher became suspicious and, as a test, he told his beloved that he would be out of town visiting his mother for the evening. Instead of departing, he hid in the projection room, watching and waiting. His suspicions were proven true when he found his girlfriend and the salesman in the balcony in a compromising position.

In a fit of rage, the boyfriend jumped to the balcony and stabbed the salesman in the shoulder, rendering his arm useless as he tried to get away. As the victim moved closer to the fire escape door, theatre patrons grabbed him, mistakenly believing that the salesman was the bad guy. When they grabbed his arm they caused further injury, until the bloody, mangled arm was barely held together by tendons. The salesman died on the fire escape over the alley.

Pandemonium broke out inside as the usher jumped from the balcony into the crowd below, breaking the neck of one patron and the shoulder of another. Eventually the usher was captured and sent to prison for life.

The salesman may still be lingering near the site of his tragic death.

"A psychic indicated that there was a male ghost hovering near the fire exit door," explained Cathy. "When people are working in the building, the door will open and close on its own. During an investigation, ghost hunters also recorded some EVPs in the balcony area."

There is evidence of other haunts at the theatre as well, namely in the basement boiler room.

"In the boiler room investigators asked the question, 'Will you tell me your name?'" said Cathy. "The ghostly reply was 'Don't want to'."

The Jayhawk Theatre was selected as the State Theatre by the Kansas Legislature in 1993 and is currently being restored to its former glory.

Columbian Building

Office workers said it sounded like a bomb explosion. Glass sprayed everywhere as the front window shattered, unexpected during a workday morning in downtown Topeka. There was one fatality, that of a young male deer.

"The buck deer had wandered from woods along the river," explained tour guide Megan Ramirez. "He roamed around downtown...when he saw his refection in the glass, he attacked it, thinking it was another male. We joke that perhaps the sound of ghostly hoof prints can be heard at the Columbian."

The Columbian building, constructed during the building boom in 1888, exemplifies the Victorian architecture of the time in the ornate exterior design. Damaged by fire in 1937, the building was threatened by demolition for years until purchased by the current owners. Renovation of the building has brought it back to its former elegant glory. Attorneys, banks, and realtors have had offices in the Columbian.

An attorney saved Carrie Nation in 1901 from an angry mob of men.

"Carrie Nation had been smashing saloons on Kansas Avenue," said Megan. "The bar patrons were upset at being disturbed, so they started to chase her down the street. She found a safe haven in the lawyer's office and then snuck out the back door to catch a train."

There are ghosts at the Columbian...one entity made an appearance in the first floor tax office.

The tax preparer's office was open one Saturday morning. It was quiet as staff waited for the first customer of the day to arrive.

"I heard footsteps in the hallway, so I walked around my desk and peeked out the doorway to see if there was a customer," said Amanda, an employee. "No one was there so I went back to my desk and sat down in my chair. When I looked up, there was a man standing in front of the desk."

A man's ghost has appeared at the tax office on the first floor of the Columbian Building.

The man was dressed in old-fashioned style clothing, including a hat and striped shirt.

"I asked if he needed assistance, but all he said was that I was sitting in his chair," continued Amanda. "I told him that this was my chair and again asked, 'do you need tax help?'"

The man walked out of her office and she followed him. No one was in the hallway.

"The one thing I noticed while he was in the office that the lights flickered," said Amanda. "I didn't feel scared, but it was a strange experience."

Other haunted activity at the Columbian includes chairs being moved during the night and cold spots in the offices. On the fourth floor a face has been seen looking out the window.

Listen closely. Does that sound like a deer walking down the sidewalk?

Field of Greens Restaurant

The bistro is popular with downtown workers who can enjoy a fresh lunch with an old haunt.

One restaurant patron watched as the trash can lid lifted up and hit the floor.

"I was standing by the salad bar, waiting in line at lunch," she said. "It surprised me to see the lid levitate, then fall on the floor."

Levitating lids are not the only evidence of a ghost. Owner Chris Schultz knows there is a haunt in his restaurant.

"I frequently see a shadow figure near the back staircase," he explained. "Most of the activity are noises and footsteps. Sometimes the cupboard doors open and close for no reason."

Staff feels the ghostly presence...it's as though someone is standing next to them or behind them.

"I was talking with a new employee, when suddenly she turned and looked behind her," Chris said. "She was expecting to see someone. I laughed and told her it was the ghost, and that she would get used to it."

Chris did notice that activity increased in the bistro after PRI spent an evening investigating.

"I think the ghost liked the attention," mentioned Chris. "After the investigators left, there were more noises and doors opening than usual."

A spirit at Field of Greens will open cabinet doors, as well as linger on the staircase.

Memorial Hall, Topeka

"Erected by the State of Kansas as a Memorial to the Union Soldiers and Sailors of the War of the Rebellion" marked the cornerstone placed by President William Howard Taft that established the Grand Army of the Republic Memorial at Tenth Street and Jackson Avenue in downtown Topeka.

Began in 1911, the official dedication ceremony took place in 1914. Attended by nearly 25,000 citizens, the building was one of the finest in Topeka. Even GAR Commander John N. Harrison was known to have commented, "Its magnificent walls of pure white marble are more eloquent than articulate speech, its very silence is impressive far beyond and above the words of man, for it assures my comrades living, that my comrades living and dead, are held in sacred memory by the great, patriotic liberty-loving people of Kansas."

The Kansas Historical Society shared the space with the GAR, filling rooms with artifacts and archives. According to historian Chris Meinhardt, "The Society stored a few of William Quantrill's bones in the basement for a while. A few years back they were turned over for burial at a Confederate cemetery."

The collections included a military room, an airplane hanging from the ceiling, and items showing how families lived on the prairie.

"As a kid I always enjoyed going to the museum," said Chris, adding, "I think it gave me a fascination for history."

The building is fascinating for another reason — *its ghosts*.

Modesto Vasquez was a security guard at the museum when he experienced the paranormal.

"Oh, there were some interesting things that happened," said Modesto. "For me the creepiest place was the military display room. From the hallway you could hear moans and cries, as though men were in pain. When anyone walked into the room, the noises would stop."

An old Victrola in one of the display rooms randomly played music, which also caught the attention of security.

"As we would make the rounds, we could hear music playing," said Modesto. "We would walk into the room and the sound would stop. Looking into the machine we could see there were not any discs inside to play. It was very strange."

Paranormal investigators have theorized that spirits can attach to people, objects, or locations. "It is possible that an entity had a special attachment to the Victrola and still enjoyed hearing the music," explained investigator Devin Cooper.

Ghostly music is heard at the Grand Army of the Republic Building.

In 1995 the museum moved to an expanded location; Memorial Hall was renovated and turned into state offices... the ghosts *did not* disappear with the collections.

"I saw a ghostly figure of a man walking the hallways," said an attorney who worked in the office. "He was a soldier, dressed in a blue uniform."

Modesto agrees, saying, "I recall seeing shadow figures in the hallway when I worked there."

Memorial Hall currently houses the offices for the state Attorney General. Although security guards at the front desk have not had their own ghost encounters, they enjoy the job.

"We work in a beautiful building full of history and character," said a guard. "I would not want to be anywhere else."

North Topeka Business District

In many ways North Topeka was settled earlier than the south side of the river. A Kaw tribe had been established for many years, and two French entrepreneurs, the Pappan brothers, operated a ferry that provided a safe crossing for travelers on the Oregon, Santa Fe, and California trails. The military road from Fort Riley to Fort Leavenworth passed nearby. By 1854, a bustling community was growing. The railroad was an important part of the growth in North Topeka, as it was a stopping point where visitors could purchase supplies and find entertainment.

Quite a few western celebrities spent time in North Topeka, including Wild Bill Hickok, William Tecumseh Sherman, George Custer, and Buffalo Bill Cody.

The notorious outlaws Bonnie and Clyde hid at some of the joints in North Topeka before they stole a car from Mrs. Ruth Warren of the Oakland neighborhood in Topeka. The gangsters were shot multiple times in the car, which is now on display at a casino in Nevada.

Natural disaster struck a blow to the area twice. Devastated by floods in 1903 and 1951, North Topeka declined in economy and population. Luckily many of the buildings still maintain their Victorian architecture, providing an historic feeling to North Kansas Avenue.

Because travelers, soldiers, and rail workers needed entertainment, vice was housed in many of the buildings. Brothels were commonly found on the second floor, alcohol and gambling could be found on the main floor, and opium dens were located in the basements. All of these activities were illegal; police were kept busy making raids, and Carrie Nation was kept busy destroying the "joints."

In 1903, the North Topeka Post Office staff used sign language and fingerpointing to communicate a lack of alcohol at their establishment. A group of Chinese railroad workers had entered the post office, thinking the building was an entertainment joint. After much persuasion, the postal clerk motioned to the workers that the drinks were plentiful down the street.

As for the ghosts, they are as unique as the district, but a common haunt is found in many of the buildings. The sounds of people having fun, partying, and laughing still linger from the past.

Brad's Corner Café

A mischievous spirit enjoys harassing the morning staff as they prepare for the day. Often the morning cook spends time alone in the kitchen, where some of the activity takes place.

"The thermostat can have problems. We set it at a temperature, but usually the building is cold when it should be warm and vice versa," he said. "I have also seen a dark shadowy figure in the back of the kitchen."

Charlie Brown's

Charlie Brown's was in business for over forty years until just recently when the bar changed hands. The current owner said he hears the sound of partying, plus other strange noises.

"We have had some deaths from alcohol poisoning and natural causes that have occurred at the bar, but they aren't haunting us," explained the owner.

He was also quick to point out that any shootings that occurred took place out front, where several people were killed during one particular incident.

The Pub

The Pub opens, and then shuts down, on a regular basis. A former manager lived in the apartment above the bar; she told us that she experienced ghost activity on the second floor.

"I would be on my bed resting and falling asleep," she said. "Sometimes the door would open slightly and I would see the face of a man peering at me through the crack."

She leapt out of bed to confront the ghostly man, but would always find the hallway empty.

"I have also heard footsteps running down the hallway to the bathroom," she explained. "One of the other tenants said a ghostly old lady has been seen upstairs...she died in the building a long time ago."

Twilighter Country Club

There is no dignity in being found dead in the bathroom. Mr. Teddy Weddle was found dead in an upstairs apartment bathroom and now his ghost is believed to haunt the front booth of the bar.

After spending most of his life in and out of prison, Teddy found comfort during his later years at the Twilighter. He often slept in the front booth; if no one lived in the apartment up-stairs, he would stay there. After he was noticed missing, staff investigated the upstairs and found that he had died; his body had gone unnoticed for several days. Now, his footsteps can be heard walking heavily down the stairs and stopping at his favorite booth at the front of the bar.

Teddy is not the only spirit in the tavern. A man and woman dressed in Victorian clothing have been seen by patrons and the manager. They glide across the room as though in conversation.

Old-timers will tell you that North Topeka joints take care of their own problems. Unless it spills into the streets, the police rarely intervene. During one incident, a man entered the Twilighter yelling and waving a gun around. This did not concern the regular patrons, who are used to such goings on. Seeing that his target was not present, the local citizen stuffed the gun into the back of his pants and sat down in the booth, ordering a beer. He sat down with a bang, since the gun went off and wounded his buttocks. One old-timer pointed out, "It is rare for the news crews to come out, so when the camera crew arrived with the ambulance we figured it must have been a slow news day."

Ward-Meade Park

One of the first pioneering families in territorial Kansas literally made a living from the Kaw River. They sold sand to early Topeka settlers.

Mary Jane Ward placed a candle in her cabin window as a method of communicating a safe haven for travelers heading west on the Oregon Trail.

The Ward-Meade house, an 1870s prairie mansion listed on the National Register of Historic Places, is the centerpiece of Old Prairie Town. The park is a replicate of a pioneer village with buildings that have been moved from other locations, such as the school and church, or created new, such as the Potwin Drug Store. The authentic environment is conducive to spirit activity.

Visitors often ask Park volunteers about haunts in the buildings; volunteers and staff have had personal experiences in several of the buildings.

Potwin Drug Store is newly built, but the memorabilia inside is old. Upstairs is a dentist office with the drug store on the lower level. Volunteers have seen a ghost in the building.

"I saw a man in a long coat standing on the outside staircase," explains a volunteer. "I also believe that the footstep sounds heard in the dentist's office upstairs is the same ghost."

It is possible that the ghost is attached to one of the many antiques in the building.

The Ward-Meade house is also haunted.

Staff and volunteers have experienced the gamut of paranormal activity, including odors, footsteps, objects being moved, voices, and shadows.

A park employee has witnessed her share of ghostly activity, including noises and doors opening and closing on their own volition.

"In the north upstairs bedroom, I saw the curtain pulled back like someone was looking out the window," said the employee. "No one was there."

In that particular room, a strong odor of rose-scented perfume drifts through the air.

It seems that one ghost of the house is able to move furniture. In the bedroom, the employee heard the distinctive sound of furniture moving, but did not think much of it. After all, staff and volunteers were in the house. Later she noticed an armoire had been moved to make space for a picture hanging on the wall. She asked staff if they had been moving furniture; they all denied moving the armoire.

Other rooms upstairs are active with spirits. During a meeting, the door in the office opened as though someone was walking into the room.

In the hallway before a tour of the house, the volunteer heard the laughter and conversations of children upstairs. The guide ran up the staircase, concerned because visitors are not allowed to walk through unattended; no children were found.

On the staircase visitors have felt something brush against their legs and heard the rustling of skirts.

The pest control man said that while he was spraying upstairs he felt someone slap his shoulder, but all he saw was an empty room when he turned around.

In one of the rooms a large doll is on display; a volunteer has seen its eyes open and close of their own volition.

"There is a theory that ghosts form attachments to dolls, perhaps because the toy is familiar to them, or because they have a human shape," said tour guide and investigator Devin Cooper.

The main floor is as active as the upper floors.

A shadow figure has been seen in the dining room and cabinet doors open and close on their own.

During the holiday season a Christmas tree stands in the parlor, beautifully decorated with numerous antique ornaments. A lower branch of the tree moves wildly up and down, as though someone was shaking it. The ornament on the tree was that of a cradle.

Staff think that a child ghost plays with the cradle, noting, "It is at the right height for a kid."

The parlor was the room where coffins and bodies were displayed before burial. After viewing a photo of the tree with an orb above it, a psychic felt that the orb was of an "old energy" that was comfortable in the space.

A psychic believes an old spirit resides in the corner of the parlor.

"We usually don't include orbs as evidence, since an orb can be spit, dust, bugs, or rain," explained Devin. "The psychic who viewed the photo is one that we trust. I believe there is an entity that resides in the parlor."

Old Prairie Town is a lovely spot to visit in Topeka, where the spirit of the Ward-Meade family still watches over their homestead.

Topeka Country Club

Generations of prominent families have enjoyed the hospitality and golf found at Topeka Country Club. Members and guests of the century-old club include Charles Curtis, vice president under Herbert Hoover, and the elite of Topeka society.

President William Howard Taft visited the club in 1911. Legendary golfers Bob Hope and Ben Hogan visited in 1944 as a fundraiser match for the war effort. Hogan and Bing Crosby visited in 1945.

However a few of the club members no longer pay their dues! Staff and patrons have seen ghosts regularly in the building and on the grounds. One of the most peculiar and active specters is a ghost named Jimmy that wreaks havoc on the second floor.

Jimmy seems fascinated by chairs.

The upstairs hallway usually has several banquet chairs lined along the wall. Nothing out of the ordinary, until one evening the general manager noticed the chairs were tipped over in a tidy row down the length of the hallway. He was uncertain as to how the chairs got that way, as no staff member ever admitted to the prank.

Fear of the ghost came to fruition while working late at night. Finished for the evening, the general manager walked down the hall, flipping light switches off on his way out of the building. The lights came back on. Disconcerted, he repeated his actions and, again, the lights came back on. The third time was unlucky — a lamp crashed against the wall, shattering onto the floor... *Jimmy the ghost?* Whatever the case, the manager moved his office to the main floor of the building and vowed not to work late or alone at the club again!

The bar features a couple of ghosts named Bob and Doc. Identified by a psychic in 2001, staff has seen their shadowy figures at a table.

However, the most common entity seen by staff and security is the ghost of a lady in 1930s attire; she has been spotted in the locker room and the lobby.

The oddest spirit — that of a rugged looking man — appears occasionally near the office area.

"He appears randomly and then dissipates," explained Cathy, "but he leaves behind a horrible indescribable stench. Staff calls him Stinky Man."

Home owners relaxing on their patios have seen misty figures dressed in 1920s style garments on the greens, as if playing a round on summer nights.

Near the tennis courts several people saw a shadow figure dart past them, moving towards the club.

Why this exclusive building is haunted with numerous spirits is unknown. Perhaps they are merely enjoying the pastimes of a previous life.

Great Overland Station

Topeka has a proud railroad heritage, exemplified at the Great Overland Station museum.

Established in 1927, the station was considered to be a crown jewel of the Union Pacific Railroad. Designed by architect Gilbert Underwood, it had ceilings rising thirty-four feet over the main lobby and elegant architectural features that were promoted nationally in Union Pacific advertising materials.

During World War II, loved ones watched as soldiers departed for battle. The station was a popular whistle-stop for politicians, including President Dwight Eisenhower.

The building itself has withstood flooding and a fire started by vagrants. Now restored, Great Overland Station is a museum and event facility.

A former maintenance man claims that several ghosts linger in the museum. One is a young woman dressed in old-fashioned clothing, who followed Carmen around while he completed his duties.

"In order to turn on or shut off the lights a special key is required," said Carmen. "Sometimes the ghost lady turned the lights off before I was ready. I asked her to turn them back on, and she did."

Carmen has also heard a woman's ghostly crying in the southwest corner of the lobby and believes it is the same woman who followed him around while he was working.

The second ghost at the station is believed to be an old ticket taker.

"In the first ticket booth the radio would start playing without being plugged in," said Carmen. "Papers and supplies would move around and drawers would be pulled out."

Other incidents took place on the balcony, where people felt as though their clothes were being tugged and their ankles pulled.

During several ghost tours guests have photographed anomalies in front of the station door.

"We call this entity ghost boy," said tour guide Megan Ramirez. "He has shown up in a few photos over the years."

A ghost boy has been seen several times in this doorway at the Great Overland Station Museum.

The first time 'ghost boy' was photographed was in the summer time during a late tour. A woman was taking a picture of her husband holding their eight-month-old baby. In the digital image was a third entity — a boy who looked to be about eleven years old with full facial features except for hollow eyes without sockets was hovering over the husband's shoulder.

The ghost was captured a second time when a group of sorority girls were taking group photos. In the image was an additional figure, a misty form shorter in height than the girls.

In subsequent tours, a mist or fog has been seen in visitor photos.

"We believe that ghost boy might have been one of those who escaped from the youth center and died while trying to catch a train," said Cathy.

Many deaths have taken place on the train tracks. In the early 1900s, two-year-old Marian Samuelson died on the tracks in a tragic accident. Her babysitter was distracted by some boys playing ball. The little girl toddled onto the tracks and was hit by a train.

The Great Overland Station Museum is a fitting location for those who are still waiting for that last train out of the station...

Curtis Family Cemetery

The Curtis Family Cemetery is a little known gem in North Topeka. The cemetery has few tombstones remaining. However, the cemetery possibly has the most activity during a tour than any other site. This small plot of land has given tour patrons experiences ranging from full body apparitions, lights, sounds, touch, and hot and cold spots.

As early founders, the Curtis family was very important in Topeka history. Senator Charles Curtis became the first and only Native American Vice President in American history under Herbert Hoover. The family buried most of their

A monument at Curtis Cemetery...notice the damage from vandals. Several ghosts haunt this graveyard.

deceased in the Curtis Family Cemetery, with the exception of Charles, who is buried at Topeka Cemetery.

Paranormal activity in the cemetery seems to occur any time and in any weather.

Three teenagers on a tour experienced hearing voices and being touched.

"I was watching three teenagers, one girl and two boys, standing in the northwest corner of the cemetery near the spot where an EVP had been recorded previously," said Devin Cooper. "It was a cold night so we had our hands in our pockets. The girl was telling the guys, 'stop trying to hold my hand'. The boys responded, 'We are not trying to hold your hand'. Moments later the other boy in the group said, 'Stop whispering in my ear'."

The incident lasted for a few seconds. The message whispered to the boy was "Where's Henry?"

The EVP that had been recorded during an afternoon investigation was "Where's Henry" in the voice of a child. The little spirit is believed to target teenage boys since numerous boys have either been touched, had their clothes tugged, or felt cold spots. On one tour for a group of 4-H kids, a boy walked into the northwest corner of the lot and was so badly frightened that he ran out of the cemetery in a panic.

Tour guide Cathy Ramirez felt something touch the top of her head while in the cemetery, and one woman actually accused a tour guide of throwing a rock at her after feeling something hit the back of her head. The guide, incredulous, asked, "Why would I throw a rock at one of our patrons?"

Noises are often heard at the cemetery. One night while showing friends some of the haunted places in Topeka, Devin and a friend approached the cemetery entrance. When they reached the front gate, the entire chain link fence started shaking, startling everyone in the vicinity. The noise had no explanation.

PRI has investigated the cemetery.

"I saw an apparition lean over the fence next to the large elm," said Nick. "I also recorded sounds of footsteps through the grass and a branch moving back and forth, as though someone was tugging at it."

Other apparitions have been seen during tours.

"While leading one group on a tour I saw a dog run past the fence," said Cathy Ramirez. "I watched the dog as it ran around, and then it just disappeared."

Over the summer of 2008 a heinous act of vandalism took place in the cemetery.

"It started like a normal tour, but as we approached we could see that the stones had been destroyed. Some were practically dust; they had been hit with a post so many times. It was a disturbing and saddening experience," explained Cathy.

"I bawled," said Devin, as she remembered seeing the destruction. "I told guides Megan and Amber that I needed to leave. I got back to the bus and cried until the tour group came back. I still cry. Curtis became special to me. It is painful to see how thoughtless people can be. I don't know who did it, but they need to know the actions that destroyed Curtis were cruel, but I won't hate them for it...I just pity them."

Rochester Cemetery

In 1857, a cemetery overlooking Kaw River was established near the town of Rochester.

"There are early settlers buried here, as well as Civil War soldiers and people who died en route to Oregon," explained Cathy. "It is an adventure into the past just to walk through the cemetery and look at the dates and names on the stones."

The town of Rochester was established by Free State settlers with hopes of becoming a metropolis.

"The idea was to become a stop on the railroad as it developed," said Cathy. "These plans did not materialize, and now all that is left of the town is a road, a school, and the cemetery."

Cemeteries often have ghost stories, and the Rochester Cemetery is no exception.

"Stories include apparitions, sounds, and lights," said Cathy. "During tours visitors have watched pinwheels spin in the pet cemetery, as well as seen a white light in the trees."

The Ghost Dog
Haley the ghost dog is popular during tours. The grave located in the pet cemetery has a pinwheel that will spin even on quiet evenings.

"We watched as the pinwheel began to move faster as our hand got closer," explained Cathy. "It was as though a little dog was wagging its tail and was happy to see us. The closer we got, the faster the wheel spun."

Haley has performed on several occasions. One evening, as Cathy and another guest visited her grave, they reached down and felt a distinct cold spot.

"We started talking to the little ghost dog, cooing, and asking Haley to play," said Cathy. "The pinwheel really started to spin!"

"Human" Ghosts

There are other ghosts at the cemetery.

"During a tour, a couple told us of their experience by the cemetery entrance, just past the bridge on Menninger Road," said Cathy.

The couple, a middle-aged husband and wife, delivered newspapers in that area and had an encounter with a ghostly jogger.

Described as being "very pale with an unusual jogging outfit, kind of a glowing fluorescent," the jogger looked as though he was jogging backwards, yet he stayed in the same place. As they approached and were parallel with him, it was an unnerving situation.

"I had pointed him out to my husband," the lady explained, "and as I looked out the window at the jogger, he looked in at us...then he disappeared."

There are also Civil War soldier ghosts.

As you enter at the top of the hill, there are three rows of Civil War soldier tombstones. "A historian who was doing research about the soldiers buried here claimed that on several occasions, she heard the sounds of soldiers marching as if going to battle. It is easy to imagine the soldiers marching to a past life," said Cathy.

Albino Lady

The most famous ghost at the cemetery — and perhaps in all of Kansas — is the Albino Lady.

"The Albino Lady was not a myth," explained Cathy. "She actually did live in North Topeka, and was very well-known in the area."

She was described as having stark, white skin, blazing pink eyes, and white, wiry hair.

"We interviewed many people who knew either the living or ghostly Albino Lady for our ghost tour of North Topeka," Cathy continued. "Their stories answer many questions."

Rochester Cemetery is home to the Albino Lady.

These are the basic details: Albino Lady lived in a small house near Rochester Cemetery. She had been employed nearby as a housekeeper for many years, as well as worked at Duckwall's Store on North Kansas Avenue. She died in 1963 and is buried in Rochester Cemetery. Because of her condition, she wore protective garments such as hats and shawls to protect her skin. Since she could not be in sunlight, she enjoyed walks in the evenings.

Larry's Story

I remember being eight years old when I would ride with my dad to pick up the Albino Lady and take her to the grocery store at Russ's IGA at Highway 24 and Kansas Avenue so she could get groceries. Normally she would walk everywhere she went. I remember sitting in the back while Dad drove and the Albino Lady sat up front. I did not know her name. I was always afraid of the way she looked. She was just as people described her: stark white skin, white wiry hair, and blazing pink eyes.

Arlene's Story

I remember walking with my older brothers and sisters through Rochester Cemetery...just to get a look at the living Albino Lady who always seemed to be hanging out there.

Michelle's Story

I was walking home with my friends and my brother when we decided to go play in the creek. While there, we looked on the bank and saw the Albino woman laughing crazily, staring at us. She scared us so much...we turned around and ran all the way home.

Middle School Teacher's Story

I saw the ghostly Albino in the cemetery in 1972. I had graduated from Seaman High School and, as a fun time with my buddies, came to the cemetery to see the Albino Lady. I actually spoke with the ghost, who had a pale German shepherd dog with her. She asked us what we were doing there; I answered that we were looking for her. The Albino Lady responded, "You boys better get going...I have to go now." I never feared for my safety except that maybe the dog could have done something if instructed.

Harvey's Story

In 1979, I came to Rochester Cemetery looking for the ghostly Albino Lady. I found her with her dog, a White German Shepherd with pink eyes. I watched as she walked across the cemetery.

Robert's Story

In 1982, I came to the cemetery to see the Albino Lady. I did see her, but got so scared I ran away as fast as I could.

Tour Bus Driver's Story

My friends took off without me when we saw the Albino Lady. I was left alone with her, but she just moved past me.

Two Girls' Story

We were driving through Rochester Cemetery on a humid evening. Every so often we would run the windshield wipers to take the moisture off of the glass. Suddenly fingers moved across the windshield, as though someone had run their hand across the glass. We were scared, and believe it was the Albino Lady.

"My sister and I attended Rochester Grade School, and are native North Topekans," said Cathy. "As a kid the first thing you learn in Kindergarten is about the Albino Lady. So many people have had a ghost experience that it's difficult to consider the story a myth."

The cemetery is closed at dusk, and the sheriff and neighbors kept a close eye out for vandals.

"One year there was a rumble here; teenage boys fighting it out in the cemetery," said Cathy. "Local law enforcement rounded them up. We take protecting the cemetery very seriously."

There are few ghosts more mysterious than Albino Lady, but be wary... she is *not* the only spirit at Rochester Cemetery.

Topeka Insane Asylum

In 1949, the new director of the State Insane Asylum had a big job on his hands. Not only was he walking into a facility that was nationally known for its intolerable living conditions and mistreatment of patients, but the hospital was also the root of a "fly menace" in Topeka.

The infamous State Insane Asylum Castle building.

The Topeka Capital reported August 12, 1949: "Immediate steps will be taken to eradicate what has been termed a fly menace at the Topeka State Hospital."

"Early this week, Johnson reported swarms of flies began infesting the area south of Sixth Street. Complaints of the fly nuisance have been pouring in all week. Conditions out there are almost indescribable."

One of the problems was that "we can kill all the flies on the surface, but as the garbage and manure piles are practically crawling with maggots, spraying does not do the job."

Over the years of its existence, open dumps and manure piles had been allowed to accumulate at the hospital. One of the recommendations was to do a "general cleanup of the grounds and dispose of garbage properly."

Garbage and flies were the tip of the iceberg of problems at the hospital.

Originally known as the Topeka Insane Asylum, the hospital had a reputation for despair and suffering. Approaching the castle-like building through the stone gates still generates a feeling of hopelessness. The turrets of the Victorian building feature bar-covered windows that convey a sinister appearance.

Today the building is collapsing on the interior; 'No Trespassing' signs cover the windows. "Demolition by Deterioration," quips most historians who have pushed to save the building as a historic landmark. Bold teenagers and reckless ghost hunters have broken into the building, hoping to capture a quick thrill or ghostly voice. A very dangerous and foolhardy endeavor, since a cry for help from an injured trespasser sounds no different from the cry of a distraught specter.

The hospital was in operation from 1872 to 1997, housing orphans, tuberculosis patients, the mentally ill, and the unwanted.

Those who were strong enough worked in the gardens, barns, and other support operations. Those who were not were tied to rocking chairs or chained to walls and the concrete slabs also used as beds. Patients were often kept in chains for years, sometimes in the nude.

"In the basement the manacles and chains still hang from the walls," noted a former pest control professional who provided service at the hospital. "The basement and tunnels were really nasty places."

Patients were test subjects for a variety of treatments, including shock therapy and drugs. There was one nurse for 1,800 patients at the hospital; when she retired there was a "staff shortage."

Ghost activity is inevitable in such an environment of human suffering.

"When I lived out by the grounds, I would take walks through the property," said Rich. "I would hear the piano playing in the front room of the castle building, even though the building was boarded up and no longer in use."

Passersby have also heard the sound of typewriters clicking away from the castle building.

"Visitors to the grounds have photographed faces peering out of the windows," said Cathy Ramirez. "During tours people have experienced anomalies as they walked around the outside of the building."

On the grounds, ghostly children have been seen at the site where the former orphanage stood.

The hospital cemetery tells the most powerful story of the neglected patients.

"Over 1,100 patients were buried in what was called the Pit," explained Cathy. "Bodies unclaimed by family members were buried in a mass unmarked grave. Very few of the graves have markers; of the nineteen with markers four are Civil War veterans."

The Topeka Public School District purchased the hospital grounds, including the castle building.

"This is one of those cases, where, as much as I like saving and preserving old buildings, its slow demise might finally release the cries of those still suffering the horrors of their incarceration," concluded Cathy.

Topeka Cemetery

Deb Goodrich wrote the book about Topeka Cemetery. Published in 1998, *Stories in Stone* documents the lives of Topekans who "chose to come here, and they found something to make them stay. In some cases, they created something to make them stay — families, businesses, political alliances. Kansas, 1854, was a place of possibilities."

During warm weather, Deb guides tours through the cemetery, pointing out notable monuments and telling stories of minutiae of lives past.

Deb wants to believe in ghosts. She has attended investigations at Constitution Hall—the most haunted building in Topeka—and she has friends who have had personal experiences with ghosts, but "thus far, I have only encountered crows" at Topeka Cemetery.

Topeka Cemetery is a favorite stomping ground for ghost enthusiasts. After all, there are over 35,000 people and 2,500 pets buried there. It is Topeka's oldest chartered cemetery.

The charter for Topeka Cemetery was granted in 1859, making it the largest organized cemetery in Kansas. Franklin Crane saw a need and initiated the charter, operating the cemetery until his death in 1884. Four generations of Cranes ran the cemetery. The original Crane home still stands, making it the oldest business building in Topeka still in use today.

The earliest cemetery in Topeka was "Old Curiosity" located at the corner of Tenth Street and Kansas Avenue downtown. Pioneers, either passing through or settling in the area, started to bury their dead there. City founders realized that the location was not a good one because the cemetery restricted commercial development downtown, so by 1860 bodies were removed and buried again at Topeka Cemetery. Although the exact number is uncertain, approximately three hundred bodies were removed over a period of two years. Over one hundred years later, two more bodies were uncovered; their remains buried in the City section of the cemetery.

"Just as you all have arrived here today, picture yourself on a Vinewood trolley that made frequent stops through these graveyard gates," said Cathy.

According to Deb, the trolley was often rented to carry caskets and mourners to the burials. "At least one driver quit. He claimed that a ghostly specter — a woman in white — crossed the tracks in front of him every night when he made his last run. A caretaker quit for the very same reason. He claimed a ghostly woman in white passed under the evergreen trees and down towards the bottoms around the outskirts of the cemetery."

"The caretaker had an experience in the Crane House," said Cathy. "He has seen a ghostly girl on the stairs. He also had lights flickering and knocks at the door with no one being there."

Another story relates to a long married couple buried in the cemetery: "Years ago the elderly wife died while in the nursing home," recalled the caretaker. "The husband was so distraught that he visited his wife's plot, laid down next to her in his future plot, and shot himself in the head."

Some people believe there are spirits here that are still seeking justice.

The first child to be murdered in Topeka was nine-year-old Edna Dinsmore. "Her body was found in a vacant building that had been torched," said Cathy. "Her hands and feet were bound and she had been horribly assaulted and murdered." Police arrested Fred Bissell, who confessed to killing Edna because Bessie, her mother, dismissed his advances.

A man named Blackhawk was the first murder victim in Topeka. He was killed by Ike Edwards.

In 1889, A. J. Rodgers, a prominent judge and business-man, was shot and killed in his home by burglar Nat Oliphant. Though Nat was secured in the newly built Topeka jail, an angry mob apprehended Nat and hanged him from the lamppost at Sixth Street and Kansas Avenue. Several days later his body was wrapped in a shroud and buried here in the cemetery.

What do all these people have in common? The killers and the victims are all buried here at Topeka Cemetery, some in unmarked graves.

"We have had our own share of ghostly occurrences while being at the cemetery," said Cathy. "During a ghost tour in October, we were getting everyone loaded up on the bus. My dad was on that tour, but he was loitering at the end of the Mausoleum section. I told him it was time to go, but he said we needed to tell the man in the coat we were leaving. With the flashlight, we went over and looked, but did not find anyone at that end of the drive. We went back to the bus, everyone was on except two people standing outside; they told me that there was a man in a coat at the south end of the mausoleums. We did a head count; everyone was accounted for. Three people saw him...they all described him as wearing a long coat and old fashioned hat, with his hands on his hips."

An anomaly was photographed in front of the railroad monument during another tour. "A tour guest was reading the inscription on the monument and his wife took his photo. On the left side of the image a misty form was exposed," said Cathy.

The cemetery closes at dusk and is gated to protect those at rest from vandals. As Deb Goodrich says in her book, "For Kansas historians, Topeka Cemetery is sacred ground."

Boys' Industrial School

Described in 1884 as "kindergarten to the state penitentiary," the Boys' Industrial School has evolved from housing mentally ill youth and orphans to being a correctional facility for violent offenders.

The cemetery that reflects the forgotten and troubled boys who lived and died at the center is located on the hill above Soldier Creek. The inmates buried their own dead; most were no older than themselves. Parents declined to claim the bodies, so the state was responsible for the burials.

Death was no stranger to the facility. Diseases such as typhoid and tuberculosis were rampant, while deaths from abuse were covered up. A boy named Barnes was forced to work in a hot kitchen while having a high fever. Perry Smith died September 8, 1888, of a heart attack at age eighteen; he was first put at the facility at age twelve for attempted rape. Several deaths were the result of hard labor, either with horses and buggies' or industrial equipment.

"Some of the boys would run away, or try to hitch a ride on a moving train," explained Cathy. "Most were seriously hurt or killed. A number of the boys in the cemetery have no cause of death listed."

Dungeons, darks cells, whipping straps, ball and chain, bread and water, and brass knuckles were all forms of punishment used on a daily basis. The boys testified that the punishment for running away was the dark cell and one meal a day. Misbehave in that dark cell and the only meal was bread and water once a day. One boy, Harry Leathers, was too weak to stand after spending two weeks in the dark cell with only bread and water.

Runaways with shackles were not uncommon. A boy named Barnett managed to escape twice. The first time he pried an iron bar off the dungeon window and made his escape. He got caught and the result was a ten-pound shackle riveted to his leg. Several days later he attempted another escape through a third-story window wearing nothing but his underwear and the shackle in the bitter cold. After several hours, he made it to his mother's house. Barnett was one of the few boys who had the courage to testify against the cruelty of the superintendent.

A state investigation in 1929 showed that boys were sometimes forced to stand naked or lay face down on their cots while being whipped.

"One hundred lashes for not being quiet was pretty standard," said Cathy. "Investigations also showed that living conditions were extremely poor for the boys while the employees were living it up large at the State's expense."

Through the years, employees of the center had their own problems, ranging from drunkenness, theft, insanity, abuse to inmates and each other, and murder. Reform school teacher J. C. Lowe murdered his wife Fanny at the facility on the morning of Sunday, June 22, 1903. He also shot himself, grazing his head.

"Fanny suffered thirty-eight hours with wounds to the abdomen," said Cathy. "On her deathbed, she wrote a note stating that it was all an accident. After three times in District Court and time spent in the insane asylum, Lowe was convicted of murder and finally sent to prison."

No ghosts linger at the cemetery...rather, they are found in the main buildings, frequently seen by staff and inmates. Regular security checks are scheduled through the original buildings of the center, most of which are no longer in use. A ghost believed to be that of Mrs. J. C. Lowe has been seen floating around the ceiling of the Arapahoe building.

"I have seen a woman in a dark dress in the Arapahoe," said a security guard. "We had heard stories of ghosts, so it was strange to actually see one."

The usual haunts have been reported at the center, including doors opening and closing, lights turning on and off, as well as the sound of children crying and whispering from the empty rooms.

Staff has also reported that a ghostly child rolls a basketball down the hallway of the main building.

"Many believe that today's ghosts are reliving the terror and abuse they endured while they lived at the institution," explained Cathy.

Bibliography/Resources

Goodrich, Tom. Bloody Dawn: The Story of the Lawrence Massacre. Kent, Ohio: Kent State University Press, 1992.

Hiebert, Debra. Stories in Stone: A sharing of the lives of some who rest in Topeka Cemetery. Topeka, Kansas: Hall Directory Printing, 1998

Reichley, John. The Haunted Houses of Fort Leavenworth. Leavenworth, Kansas: Fort Leavenworth Historical Society, 1995.

Russell, J.R. "Old Mansion Filled with Legend." Kansas City Kansan, June, 29, 1975.

Schott, Cindy and Kathy Schott Gates. Boys, Let Me Down Easy. Lawrence, Kansas: Allen Press, 2005.

Newspaper Articles

† "A Fearful Fall." Topeka Daily Capital, July 27, 1890.

† "Burned at the Stake." New York Times, January 6, 1901.

† "Ghost Child." Atchison Globe, January 3, 1878.

† "Ghost Stalks Abroad." Lawrence Journal World, November, 26, 1897.

† "Murder and Lynching." The Weekly Special, Vol. XXII, March 29, 1899.

† "Promises Action on Hospital Fly Menace." Topeka Daily Capital. August 12, 1949.

Index